December 1998

Amy & Bob –
   May your gardens always
by half as beautiful as these ...
   Merry Christmas
          love
Penny, John, Emily, Jack & Peter

A Passion for Flowers

A Passion *for* Flowers

By Carolyne Roehm

DESIGN BY
DOUGLAS TURSHEN
PHOTOGRAPHY BY
SYLVIE BECQUET, ALAN RICHARDSON
MELANIE ACEVEDO, FRANÇOIS HALARD

HarperCollins*Publishers*

for Grandma

The first days of spring are a gift to the spirit. When the daffodils explode, the garden is a constant and ever-changing source of *joy!*

PAGE 12

The sounds and smells of summer intoxicate—in this glorious carefree time one's spirits are high, but—the work is endless.

PAGE 114

We can revel in the amazing **colors,** *the sound of rustling leaves, and the smell of wood smoke from the first fires of* autumn. *The senses are assaulted.*

PAGE 168

The first snowfall of the season is as **exciting** *as the first crocus that comes to light at the end of* winter.

PAGE 218

**OTHING LIGHTS UP A ROOM LIKE FLOWERS.** A strategically placed bouquet has the power to create a mood and make us feel special. We use flowers in massive numbers to celebrate the most important occasions in our lives and in tiny nosegays to brighten a gloomy day. The return of flowers in the spring, after the harshness of winter, is always a miraculous event. Flowers give beauty, color and fragrance, strength and continuity, in a world that is increasingly difficult, hectic, and often indifferent. When flowers give us pause, and we consider them in all their glory, if only for a moment, we taste the sublime. Our reactions to flowers are so powerful that flowers must possess many of the qualities our souls long for.

As a child in rural Missouri, one of my favorite pastimes was to play "florist" during summer visits to my grandmother's home. Her farm—with mounds of Red Blaze roses, rows of hollyhocks, stalks of towering sunflowers, and patches of sunny marigolds—gave me plenty of fodder to create one bouquet after another.

My grandmother also helped me to understand and appreciate the unique relationship that flowers have with their containers and how each should enhance the beauty of the other. I learned that the strong and bright colors of country flowers—such as zinnias and dahlias—look best in big earthenware jugs and farm baskets, and that delicate, diminutive flowers like violets and lilies of the valley are wonderful in a tiny silver vase or a pale vaseline glass bowl.

I think of flowers in the same way that I think of fashion design—in terms of color, texture, composition, taste, style, and budget. Just as haute couture is exclusive and expensive, certain flowers are extremely rare and costly. But there are even more beautiful varieties that are affordable, and others that are so overused that they are no longer considered fashionable—yet if properly used become chic.

Flowers are by no means limited to those who enjoy great wealth or rank. As a fledgling assistant starting out in my career and earning $126 a week, there was no money to indulge myself. Still, I always managed to have one or two cut flowers in a small vase at home. Such an arrangement cost very little, yet lasted the week, and improved my quality of life enormously. Even today I enjoy bouquets that are simple and budget-conscious in addition to more opulent arrangements.

I had the great fortune to work as an assistant to designer Oscar de la Renta, the person I most admired

our souls long for.

in the New York fashion world. For an aspiring fashion designer, it was an opportunity of a lifetime. In the ten years that I worked with Oscar, I not only learned about clothes, I learned about life beyond the white fences of my simple upbringing—especially about the vital role of flowers in making life more joyous.

I learned the most about flowers from Oscar on visits to his country home, where I absorbed his enthusiasm for the gardens there and his vision for making them a visual masterpiece of plants and flowers. Travel exposed me to the riches of blooms the world over, such as the extraordinary roses of Isola Bella, the beautiful Agnelli garden designed by Russell Page, the surprising white gardens and moss gardens of Japan, and boatloads of marigolds and jasmine headed for market in Kashmir.

My fashion business frequently took me to Paris, where my passion for flowers was nurtured. I always stayed at a hotel near the Place de la Madeleine, home to countless flower stalls. I loved to stroll through the market, reveling in the selection of fresh blooms. I brought flowers back to my room, including violet bouquets for my bedside. The flowers of Paris have been a constant source of joy and wonderment and enlightenment for me. For that reason, when I began working on this book, I went straight to Henri Moulie, one of the most respected and creative florists in Paris, to learn some of the tricks of the floral trade as his apprentice.

As you will see as you turn these pages, my flower style is very simple and straightforward. I do not espouse overly "arranged" compositions and do not care to use totally disparate elements together such as peppers and roses. Although this eclectic mix of elements is rather popular with professional florists, making a vase out of asparagus spears is

just not my thing. I prefer to stick with a musty terra-cotta pot or a piece of old porcelain.

I hope this book will help you draw the same uplifting and pleasurable experiences from flowers that I have enjoyed. For convenience, I decided to organize the book by season. I have included a list of flowers and other vegetation that I enjoy during each of these periods at the beginning of each section. Please keep in mind that I do my planting and gardening at my home in Connecticut. The weather that I experience there (the late springs and early frosts) do temper these lists—you may want to adjust them accordingly. The book is meant to take advantage of the flowers that come into their glory in every season, as captured in the inspiring images of the gifted photographers who worked with me.

The book is full of ideas for brightening holidays and other special occasions with flowers, and for bringing flowers into our everyday world in special ways as well. Throughout the book I have included bouquet recipes, with lists of "ingredients" and practical, step-by-step instructions for blending them into beautiful arrangements. I have also provided short sections exploring three important themes that I mention throughout: elements of style, containers, and the basics on conditioning.

Remember, there are no wrong arrangements, just ones that work better, brighten your spirit more, or captivate your guests' rather than overwhelm them. The most important thing to keep in mind when creating bouquets and developing your artistic eye is to have fun and enjoy your masterpiece for as long as it lasts.

Spring

"I have always had a

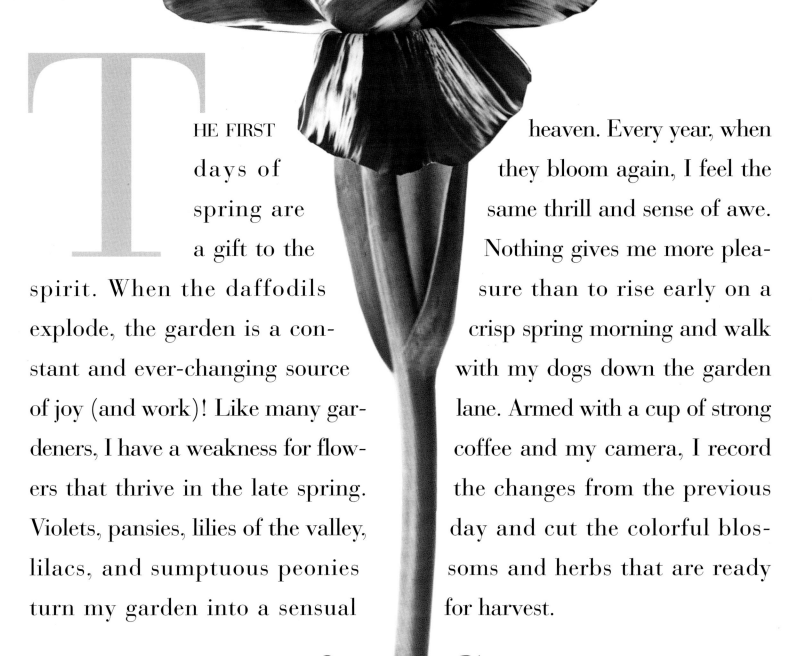

T HE FIRST days of spring are a gift to the spirit. When the daffodils explode, the garden is a constant and ever-changing source of joy (and work)! Like many gardeners, I have a weakness for flowers that thrive in the late spring. Violets, pansies, lilies of the valley, lilacs, and sumptuous peonies turn my garden into a sensual heaven. Every year, when they bloom again, I feel the same thrill and sense of awe. Nothing gives me more pleasure than to rise early on a crisp spring morning and walk with my dogs down the garden lane. Armed with a cup of strong coffee and my camera, I record the changes from the previous day and cut the colorful blossoms and herbs that are ready for harvest.

passion for flowers..."

bleeding hearts

columbines

daffodils

hellebores

hyacinths

irises

lilacs

lilies of the valley

muscari

narcissus

pansies

peonies

ranunculus

tulips

viburnum

violets

april in paris

I WORKED IN A FLOWER SHOP DURING MY FIRST spring in Paris. Because of my apprenticeship I was encouraged to frequent Runjis, the extraordinary wholesale market in France. The market was a sight to behold with row after row of gorgeous flowers bursting in color, quality, and size that I had never seen before. In addition, the ambience of this market was warm and friendly, with an easy familiarity and camaraderie between vendors and buyers. These gentle men and women of the flower world made their work even more pleasurable by sharing a cup of coffee; a lunch of a baguette, saucisson, and cheese; or just a glass of wine.

The most beautiful and hopeful season of the year envelops us after the long and dreary winter months. Soft colors in all the spring blooms conjure visions and sensations of early spring days. No more dark, heavy coats—just a sweater, a sense of lightness, and the feeling that everything is possible.

I chose this floral color palette to enhance the painted urns' celadon, gold, and soft greens. Arrangements should be created with their surroundings and containers in mind. The more you consider the total picture, the stronger the statement you will make.

The apricot and celadon of parrot tulips and the double pink tulip Angelique are so pretty with coral and peach ranunculus and paperwhites. In the center bouquet, clusters of a medium-blue violet muscari contrast with the soft, warm palette of apricots, pinks, and corals. In the two side bouquets, a mint green hydrangea and white anemones are added. The two pictorial urns are planted with small yellow rosebushes and blanketed with moss.

FLOWERS SAY SO MUCH. THEIR COLOR, form, combination, and container tell a story and create a mood. The attitude of a room changes completely with different colors and flowers. The bright blue and purple (see pages 28–29) communicate a completely different feeling from the soft peaches, apricots, and greens used in these graceful bouquets.

These beautiful and feminine roses and ranunculus are soft and sensual. Although these flowers look fragile, in fact, they are not. The rose Ambience lasts a full two weeks with a little care and conditioning, and the ranunculus lasts more than a week.

What could be more feminine

than *delicate* apricot ranunculus?

For a spring dinner in Paris I select green and white as my basic color scheme. Starting with a tablecloth cut from excess curtain fabric, I use a sage green wire basket of spring flowers as a centerpiece. White narcissus, campanulas, purple hues of muscari and pansies, and soft greens of Snow Ball viburnum impart a sense of spring with their light, fresh colors. White porcelain vases of purple pansies and blue-violet muscari surround this large central bouquet.

Fragile flowers in soft luminous

colors create spring magic.

I N FRANCE I ENJOY WAN-
dering among the fruit
carts, vegetable vendors,
fishmongers, and huge
stands filled with grilled
chickens, sausages, and meats. The
Parisian food markets always
include one or two flower mer-
chants in this gastronomic heaven,
and I can't resist purchasing my
everyday flowers from them a
couple mornings a week. Flowers,
like food, are part of daily exis-
tence for the French. With their
intuitive awareness of quality, they
know that no meal is complete
without the eye being fed as well.

Recently I bought flowering
plum branches, ranunculus, and
pink hydrangea at the market
and found these rusty old iron
urns the perfect contrast. The urns
are reproductions that can easily
be found, aged, and afforded, and
they contribute enormously to the
overall look of the composition.
Notice how the pink silhouettes
against the celadon walls, and
the arching effect of the plum
branches enclose the bouquet of
hydrangea and ranunculus to
give a finished look.

A few sprigs of broom, a healthy portion of patterned ranunculus, and some fragrant creamy yellow double freesias compliment this small golden vase. A scarf on the table ties together the colors in the flowers with the rest of the room.

When I see genêt (or "broom") I immediately think of France and big bushes swaying along the roads of Provence. I love the graceful arching manner of this flowering shrub. A big bunch of it in a vase or a basket, and the room fills with spring.

HEN ENTERTAINING, I visualize my home as a stage and try to create an ambience that flows from room to room. There are many factors in orchestrating a mood and a memorable evening. The season influences both menu and decor. The choice of music, lighting, the scent in the air, and what rooms will be used for cocktails, dining, coffee, and after-dinner drinks must foster a sense of hospitality and warmth.

Purple anemones, freesia, muscari, blue shaded with green hydrangea, and a stronger green viburnum create a monochromatic palette. This color scheme is created from the cool end of the color spectrum with blues, violets, and greens. To add spice I brought in a beautiful yellow rosebush (not pictured) and added a rose or two from the bush to the array of cut flowers. This produces a vibrant complementary color scheme (yellow and violet) and blends both cut and living flowers.

Sweet peas
are a source of sensual
gardening joy with their
ravishing iridescent
colors and fragile
rufflelike blooms…

BUT, ALAS, I HAVE TRIED unsuccessfully to grow them for years. I've read. I've studied. I've experimented. But to no great success. No place on earth has the variety, the range of color, and the quality that the French sweet peas have. I don't know how they grow such long stems and huge blooms, but I buy armfuls of them during every trip.

The array of colors and the beauty of sweet peas are remarkable—and despite their delicate appearance, they are surprisingly hearty and long-lasting.

Sweet peas in analogous colors of soft yellows, warm pinks, and corals imply femininity.

These sweet peas
in shades of violet—
the coolest range
of colors—are
irresistibly beautiful.

WHEN I DECORATED MY SMALL apartment in Paris, I decided to create a totally feminine eighteenth-century haven. I have always been intrigued with that period in French history: the great courtesans, the decorative arts; the use of color; the magic of the artisans in embroidery, fabric, china, furniture, book-making, architecture, music, and the other arts.

The cerise sweet peas and ranunculus pick up the pinks in an eighteenth-century fabric design I used on my bedroom wall. A couple of Rembrandt and par-rot tulips give texture to the bouquet. In the smaller silver vase the cerise roses, peony tulips, and ranunculus are the same color but in different hues and tints.

Normally I place the most delicate flowers last, but in this case the stronger stem of the sweet pea creates a structure on which I add the twisting soft ranunculus. The Rembrandt tulips are inserted last to ensure they are properly placed for a balanced bouquet.

I am a devotee of Parisian flea markets, and I found my eighteenth-century bed at the Marché aux Puces. The bed is framed by two containers of sweet peas, ranunculus, and parrot tulips.

For the large silver pitcher: 30 cerise sweet peas, 40 light pink sweet peas, 15 cerise ranunculus, 9 ranunculus buds, 6 white and red violet Rembrandt tulips. For the smaller bouquet: 10 cerise roses, 10 cerise (peony) tulips, 4 ranunculus buds.

I FIND CHARTREUSE A PERFECT FOIL FOR SO
many colors, from cool to hot to soft pastels
to pure white. While there are not a lot of
chartreuse flowers, viburnum is one that is
both pretty and versatile. Of course color
preference is entirely subjective, but I love combin-
ing that brilliant green with rich, velvety, purple
pansies and violets. I often mix complementary plants
and flowers to create a still life. The plant here is a
beautiful clematis called Gypsy Queen, which echoes
the purple of the pansies and violets.

Three shades of purple mingle with beautiful
cerise ranunculus in a glorious burst of color. The
pansies and violets are pre-tied into nosegays, and
some of the ranunculus are gathered into small
bunches. As the vermeil 1930s ice bucket is shallow,
I use a pick frog in the bottom to hold all of these
delicate stems (oasis does not work well when the
stems of flowers are delicate or small). Insert the
clusters of flowers to form the bouquet and fill in
with single stems of ranunculus wherever a shot of
cerise is desired.

NARCISSI ARE NATURE'S SUPREME song of hope and joy. Whether naturalized in a meadow, pushing up in strategic corners of a border, or sprouting in containers in the home, daffodils bloom just when many of us have had our fill of the long and colorless winter. I began planting daffodils (which mercifully the deer do not eat!) during my first months at Weatherstone. Years later—after adding a few more bulbs each fall and because of their naturalization process—I now have two fields of delightful daffodils. These flowers are the original happy faces, but they smile at us in many different ways, from trumpet daffodils such as the famous King Alfred, to the long- and short-cupped varieties such as Mrs. Backhouse (the world's first pink daffodil), to the cheery garden jonquils as sweetly scented as they are durable. I love to gather freshly cut bunches of daffodils from my garden, the more the merrier, and display them with ones growing in pots. Their availability, affordability, and sunny blooms more than compensate for their short life span.

The skies can't keep their secret! They tell it to the hills—The hills just tell the orchards—And they the

HANS MEMLING
INGRES

daffodils!

—Emily Dickinson

easter

OR EASTER SUN-
day, shimmering
cut glass makes a
sparkling show-
case for these
expressive daffodils and allows
their nodding beauty to shine
through, from slender green stalks
to sunny blossoms. Per French cus-
tom, I cover a footed crystal bowl
with a tender bed of grass and
pepper it with goose eggs gathered
from the local fromagerie. If goose
eggs are not available, tuck the
naturally colored eggs of free-range
hens into the edible rough.

CARE

*Daffodils leak a sap that greatly
shortens the life span of other
flowers. Therefore, before using them
in an arrangement with other
flowers, cut the stem and hold it over
a candle or gas flame to sear
the end and stop the flow of sap.*

*When buying daffodils always
opt for the tighter, more closed buds.
Open daffodils have a relatively
short life span.*

N ARCISSI AND
blue forget-me-nots symbolize
spring to me, and their juxtaposition produces a bold but delicate
effect. A reproduction Victorian
wire basket reinforces the room's
green-and-white theme and is
shallow enough to keep the flowers below eye level. The spherical
centerpiece, along with the miniature vases at each place setting,
softens the pattern in the taffeta
tablecloth.

HOW TO: A SPRINGTIME CENTERPIECE

*6 bunches forget-me-nots
(each bunch should contain roughly
20 sprigs with multiple flowers)*

8 bunches daffodils (varied)

*Green florist string (or rubber bands
or plastic bag twist ties)*

Several large leaves of ivy

*1 large metal pick frog
to fit container*

1. Remove the leaves from the flower stems. Assemble the flowers in small bouquets, 4 to 5 inches in diameter, tying them with the florist string.

2. Cut the stems so that the bouquets stand just above the rim of the container. The bouquets for the center of the container should be cut slightly taller so that the finished piece appears slightly convex.

3. Finish each bouquet by surrounding it with ivy leaves and securing them with string.

4. A metal frog placed in the bottom of the container allows each bouquet to be positioned securely.

5. Arrange the bouquets in alternating colors and shapes, working around the circumference of the container and then filling in the center.

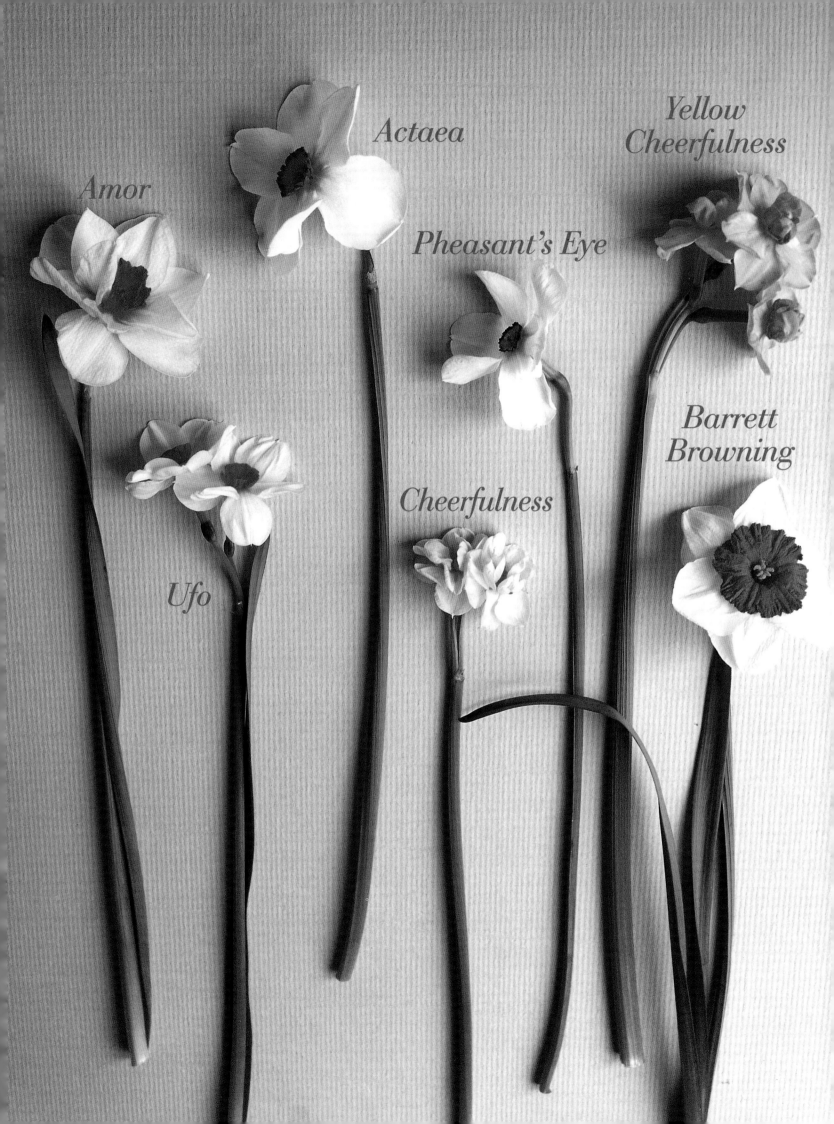

Amor

Actaea

Yellow Cheerfulness

Pheasant's Eye

Barrett Browning

Cheerfulness

Ufo

I CANNOT RECALL IF I FIRST NOTICED PARROT tulips in nature and then noticed them in Dutch flower paintings or vice versa. Their exuberant coloring and wild painterly appearance have made them a favorite in both my garden and my home over the years.

Most flower lovers know the story of tulipmania in seventeenth-century Holland, when fortunes were invested and often lost in the precious bulbs. Nowadays most of us aren't ready to mortgage our houses for them, but I have never heard of anyone who dislikes tulips. Their variety of shapes and colors is wonderful and vast. Tulips brighten the winter months as we force bulbs and ship them in from Holland, France, and even Washington state. It's amazing what a dozen tulips in a simple glass vase do to brighten a room and one's spirits.

Waves of tulips bloom from the third week of May until the middle of June in my garden. Painted Rembrandt tulips, classic tulips, and parrot tulips in an array of hues from pure white to the almost purple-black of the tulip Queen of the Night make my spring cutting garden an explosion of color.

From the soft apricots and celadon to the explosive red and yellow, painted or parrot tulips create such vitality in any bouquet that I much prefer them to the more traditional solid varieties. For this reason, I generally plant the more unusual varieties in my garden and supplement them with the more common tulips readily found in the local flower market.

I have never heard of anyone who dislikes

tulips

Esther Rijnveld tulip

Viking tulip

Coral Double tulip

Red Parrot tulip

Judith tulip

S INCE THE DUTCH became the masters of tulip production, it stands to reason that they would also devise a special vase, called a tulipier, for showing off their prized flowers. I love working with these unusual vases, but they do require a certain amount of patience, as the stems of tulips so love to twist and turn to the light. When the stems are cut short, they can become quite unruly, but that is also part of their charm in these porcelain pyramids.

Tulipiers are not easily found, but this same combination of tulips is just as effective in a small glass vase. The corals, roses, oranges, and hints of yellow and green in this combination of classic, parrot, and peony tulips make this bouquet pop.

I perhaps owe becoming a

painter to flowers. *—Claude Monet*

CARE OF TULIPS

Cut away any white portion of the stems, as tulips (along with hyacinths and daffodils) cannot absorb water through this barrier.

You can control the look of the tulip by the amount of water it is given. For arching, dancing, moving tulips, put a small amount of water in the bottom of the vase. For a straighter, more uniform look, fill the container full of water—the stems will absorb it and stiffen.

To perk up drooping tulip heads, make a tiny incision in the stem of the tulip just beneath the part where the petals attach. This releases any air locked in the neck of the flower.

To resurrect limp tulips, cut the stems (preferably under water) and roll the bunch within a column of paper. Place them in a bucketful of room-temperature water for a few hours. They will absorb the water and become little tin soldiers.

For a spring outdoor luncheon I cut an array of mixed parrot tulips in red and white and match them with a traditional checked table cloth. I love the graphic mixture of these different painted and parrot tulips as they create a bouquet that has movement and vibrancy. A friend gave me these handsome red plastic glasses and plates, which I use outside. They look great — and no worries about breakage!

Whether in the casual outdoor
setting of a weekend picnic
or a classic formal English
porcelain vase, the magic of
the different patterns and
shapes of tulips is apparent.
This arrangement contains
three different types of parrot
and painted tulips—the
differences in the patterns and
shapes are subtle, but
give the bouquet panache.

The earth laughs in flowers.

— *R. W. Emerson*

BLACK TULIPS ARE really deep maroon and provide a rich foil for so many other colors. In this case soft yellow double freesias and beautiful maroon-bordered ranunculus bounce beautifully off these deep dusky tulips.

This particular bouquet reminds me of my days in the fashion business, when I spent hours working with an Irish woolen mill to invent unusual and vibrant tweed combinations. The celadon-and-cream-striped taffeta walls provide a pretty background for this French urn and echo the color in the arrangement.

FRENCH URN

1 dozen Queen of the Night tulips

1 dozen black parrot tulips

8 President Kennedy tulips (orange-yellow)

2 dozen creamy yellow double freesias

2 dozen painted ranunculus

1. Place the majority (but not all) of the tulips in the vase.

2. Weave the freesia through the tulips.

3. Fill in with the ranunculus.

4. Finally, add the remaining tulips wherever you see the need for balance and weight.

I WAS BORN IN MAY, AND MY GRANDMOTHER always decorated my birthday cake (usually angel food with white fluffy icing) with the spring violets from her farm. It is no wonder then that violets have always held a special place in my heart and have even had a significant presence in my designing career. I have embroidered violets on ball gowns and pinned silk ones on hats and jacket lapels. Because of the fashion business I traveled several times a year to Paris, where a nosegay of violets can be purchased for twenty francs. I often trotted over to the Place de la Madeleine to buy two or three of them for my hotel room.

The pansy is another flower that I find totally irresistible. Their exquisite velvet faces are completely charming, and they grow in such a variety of colors and markings. I use pansies as an under-planting for my pink, apricot, and yellow rose gardens. In late May I often return home after an outing to the nursery with my Jeep filled with flats of pansies. Not all of them make it to the garden, though, as I fill baskets and terra-cotta pots with the plants to decorate my house and porch.

I never saw pansies used as a cut flower until I lived in France. Just outside of Paris small growers gather clusters of pansies and patiently wrap ivy leaves around each nosegay à la Eliza Doolittle. En masse at the Paris market these adorable miniature bouquets are quite breathtaking and memorable. In the past I had used potted pansies, violets, and violas in either old terra-cotta pots or some of my blue-and-white porcelain to decorate tables in the country, but I have now incorporated them into my cut-flower repertoire as well.

pansies, Johnny-jump

ups, violets, violas

INCE PANSIES ARE
not traditionally
used as cut flowers
on this side of the
ocean, at Weather-
stone I buy plants and cut my
flowers from them. Look for a
plant with the most buds form-
ing. After you trim the flowers for
your bouquet, you can place the
plant with its remaining buds in
the garden and enjoy the continu-
ous blooms for another four to six
weeks. While this sumptuous flower
appears to be quite delicate, the cut
pansy lasts as long as a week.

A less formal version of this
purple, white, and clear-glass setting can easily be attained by
replacing the antique crystal with
modern glass. Suppliers such as
Crate & Barrel, Pier 1 Imports, and
Pottery Barn have simple but good-
looking containers and dinner ser-
vices that would work nicely.

**The deep velvety purple and lilac
pansies make a beautiful contrast to
glistening crystal and a shimmery
white cotton piqué tablecloth. In the
center of the table a large cut-
crystal bowl is filled with ten small
bouquets of pansies, while wine
carafes containing one nosegay apiece
are sprinkled around the settings.**

TO MAKE A PANSY NOSEGAY

10 to 12 pansies, green florist string, ivy or galax leaves

1. Cut the pansies with as long a stem as possible and gather them carefully into a small, round cluster. Tie with green florist string.

2. Clip the stem ends so they are uniform in length.

3. Surround each cluster of pansies with 5 large ivy or galax leaves that overlap one another to frame the flowers.

4. Secure the leaves with more string.

TO MAKE THE LARGE CENTERPIECE

1 pick frog, 10 pansy nosegays

1. Place a pick frog in the bottom of a container. The pansy stems are so short that a shallow bowl works best.

2. To give the centerpiece a slightly rounded look cut 4 of the 10 individual bouquets slightly longer (1 to 1½ inches).

3. Position the tallest pansy nosegays in the center of the container and fill in around the sides with shorter nosegays to create a graceful dome shape (trim stems as necessary to produce this form). Alternate shades of purple in a pretty ombré pattern.

W E ALL NEED TO BE PAMPERED every so often. Women in particular are so busy creating a comfortable environment for friends and family that they often forget to consider themselves. Whether your idea of a treat is soaking in a fragrant bubble bath or taking a leisurely walk after dinner, it is important to allow ourselves such niceties. For instance, I love pretty breakfast, luncheon, and tea trays. Even if I am just eating a baked potato in front of the TV, I set my tray with nice silver, pretty linen, a small vase of flowers, and candles. Why not? It requires minimal effort and makes the meal much more enjoyable.

For afternoon tea in the spring, LEFT, a basket tray with a vase of Johnny-jump-ups gives a boost to one's energy and spirits.

The combination of violets, pansies, white embroidered linen, and sunny lemons makes a pretty still life for a dresser or side table in a guest room.

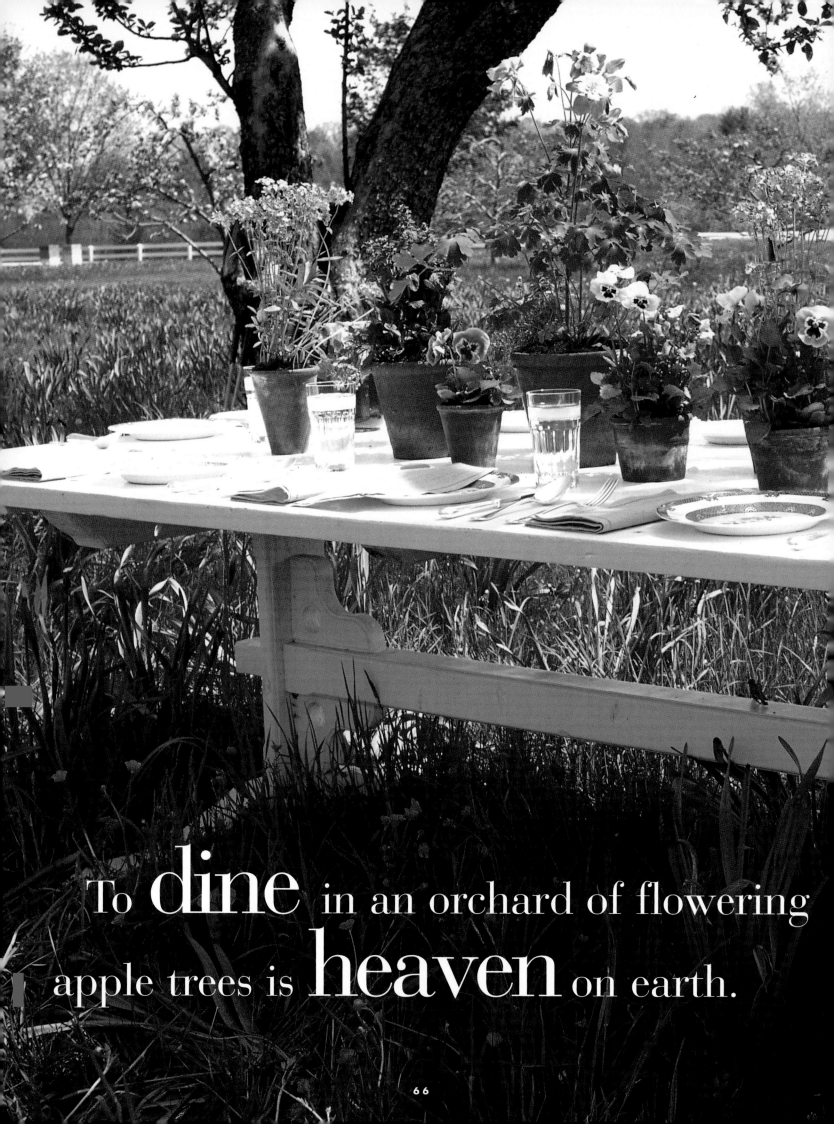

To **dine** in an orchard of flowering apple trees is **heaven** on earth.

I LOVE DINING UNDER MY flowering apple trees. For years I have planted thousands of daffodil bulbs around their trunks. The sea of yellow and white is a beautiful background for a late spring luncheon with potted pansies, columbine, and Jacob's ladder. All those pretty lavenders and violets make the table so fresh and springlike.

Old terra-cotta pots have much more charm and character than the mass-produced pots available in the stores. In the early spring I make several trips to the nursery and load up on a huge selection of pretty flowering plants. I'm always anxious to get them home and transplant them into some of my favorite aged pots.

HOW TO TRANSPLANT

Pansy plants

Aged terra-cotta pots

Potting soil

Sheets of moss

1. Remove the plants from their plastic containers and position within the terra-cotta pot.

2. Add potting soil as needed and a little fertilizer.

3. Surround each of the plants with pieces of moss to give them a pretty, finished look and help them retain moisture. I often use moss that I scrape off my damp basement wall, but you can also purchase it at your local florist. An attractive alternative to fresh moss is dried processed moss.

Hyacinths, sweet peas, carnations, lilacs—

The cool end of the color spectrum is refreshing and beautiful. These arrangements in inexpensive blue-and-white vases look like the essence of spring. I often cluster small vases containing different flowers. Only a small number of flowers are used, and yet the overall effect makes a tremendous impact.

such delicious intoxicating smells.

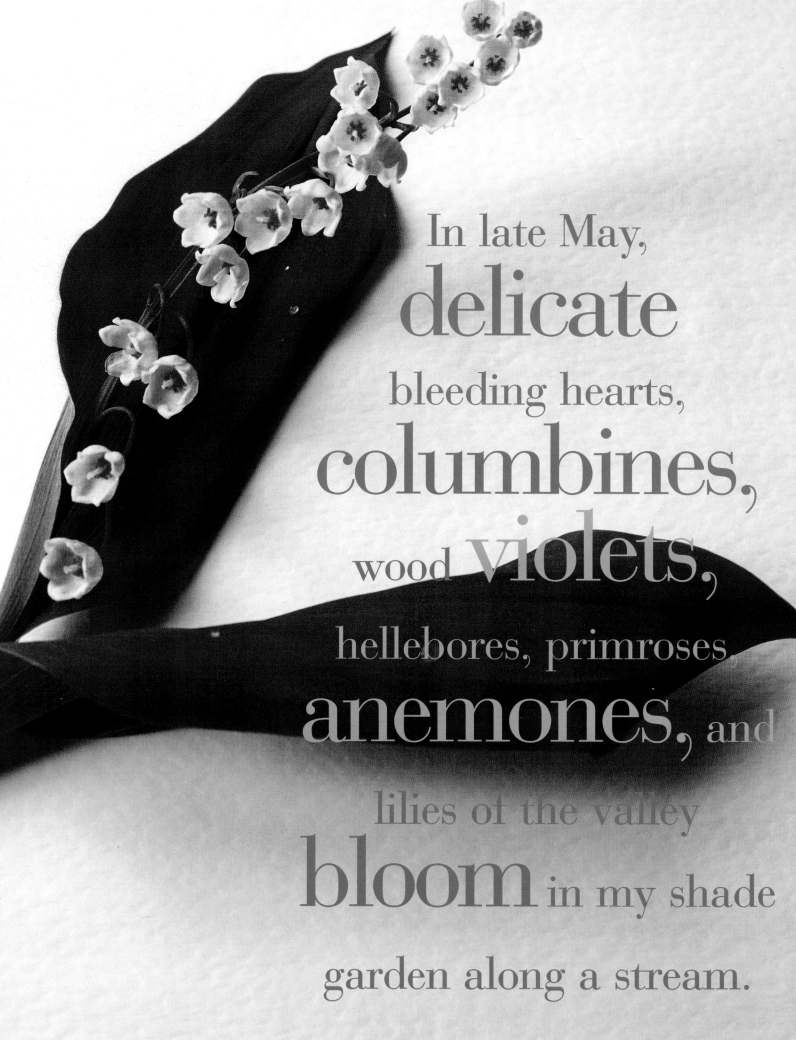

In late May,
delicate
bleeding hearts,
columbines,
wood violets,
hellebores, primroses,
anemones, and
lilies of the valley
bloom in my shade
garden along a stream.

mother's day

THE THEME OF silver, green, and white is so fresh and springlike. I adore lilies of the valley both as potted plants (which last much longer) and as cut flowers. For Mother's Day, the mixture of silver, crystal, French white porcelain, and terra-cotta pots gives the effect of having a small formal garden inside. In the center of the table, double white tulips in a large fluted terra-cotta pot trail cuttings of variegated ivy among the potted and cut lilies of the valley.

Lily of the Valley

Bleeding Heart

Hellebore

Anemone

Luscious green and white flowers sparkle in this small satin glass vase my grandmother gave me years ago.

The bouquet of spring flowers is not very large but it still has great impact on a luncheon table. The arching bleeding hearts, white columbine, graceful white *Anemone sylvestris* and a few stems of lilies of the valley mix with vivid green hellebores.

T HE MIXTURE OF DEL-
icate white flowers in a variety of
silver vases is so simple and pretty.
With the exception of the 1930s
ice bucket (holding the lilies of
the valley) all of these containers
are very affordable reproduction
silver plate.

These beautiful white flowers
have such individual shape and
character. The delicate sweet peas
and lilies of the valley join white
anemones, pheasant's eye narcissi,
white pansies, and a small plant
of *Anemone blanda* to create a
lovely tableau. In addition, the
fragrances of several of these white
flowers are the essence of spring.

Sapphire Hills, Wayside Lyric, Mary Frances, and Cheriage Lace compose this bouquet of irises in an old English creamware soup tureen.

iris

1

BEARDED GERMAN IRISES REMIND ME OF my childhood. We had a swath of these fragile flowers in the backyard and despite the little attention that was ever paid to them, they returned year after year. The furry velvety "falls" against the tissue-paper frills of the petals are breathtaking. I am starting to add more irises in my garden because of their spectacular colors. Sadly, they do not last long after they've been cut, but in the interim they are truly wonderful.

CONDITIONING TIPS

Cut German irises when a maximum number of buds have unfurled. Add one teaspoon of sugar per each quart of water in the vase.

1. Swaths of purple and lavender Iris siberica *border my pond. Occasionally I cut a few stems, but I know that they will only last two to three days. The bearded German irises in the perennial garden endure slightly longer.*
2. The iris Lyric has an apricot-yellow center surrounded with burgundy frills. 3. Two or three of these magnificent irises make a charming bouquet. 4. The translucent beauty of Rare Treat (white with purple edge), Gay Parasol (pale lavender with deep purple lower petals), and Sapphire Hills irises is remarkable. Those luscious shades of violets are lovely in a deep amethyst glass vase. 5. These beautiful purples, violets, pinks, and yellows are the predominant color theme in my perennial garden. 6. The Sapphire Hills iris has a graceful shape.

4

Sometimes as I wander around my property in Connecticut, I gather flowers and weeds growing wild in the fields and randomly pick from the shade and cutting gardens. Back home I arrange my spoils haphazardly in Mason jars and display them wherever I need simple bursts of color.

JAR 1

ox-eye daisy

columbine

wild yellow weed

JAR 2

clover

*geranium
psilostemon*

JAR 3

*blue sapphire iris
(violet)*

*laced cotton iris
(white and yellow)*

*rare treat iris
(dark purple edges)*

*tangerine dream iris
(orange)*

*moon journey iris
(yellow)*

JAR 4

*geranium
himalayense*

columbine

*rose blanc double
de coubert*

JAR 5

queen anne's lace

*magenta and
lavender wild phlox*

Charles
Joly

Dwight D.
Eisenhower

Mme.
Lemoine

lilac

For an early summer lunch on the terrace I assemble a huge bowl of my old French lilacs. Since these are heavy flowers, I place a ball of chicken wire or a large block of heavy oasis in the bottom of the vase before inserting the lilacs. The neutral colors of the table linens, flatware, and service accentuate the explosion of beautiful lilacs in the center of the table.

A N OLD HEDGE-row of traditional American lilacs borders South Main Street in the small historic town of Sharon, Connecticut. From my second-story windows I can watch these swaying heads of lilac and inhale their intoxicating scent. At twilight the beautiful reddish violet lilacs stir against the coral, pink, and golden orange sky in a gentle lullaby as the town prepares for bed.

At the back of the vegetable and cutting garden I have a row of old lilac. Many of these antique varieties are French and the colors range from white to a pale bluish lilac to a medium-intensity red-violet, to lavender, to deep rich purple.

CONDITIONING TIPS

Cut lilacs when approximately one half of the flower buds are open. Scrape the bottom 2 inches of bark off the stem and then slit this part of the stem two or three times. Lilacs respond well to 120°F to 150°F water. A floral preservative really extends the durability and buoyancy of lilacs.

At **lilac time** I fill the house and porch with bowls and baskets of lilacs.

Starting at the end of May,
I virtually live on the porch at
Weatherstone. It is one of
my favorite places to entertain
my friends, enjoy good food,
and display wonderful flowers.
 The roses almost glow against
the lavender and purple lilacs
as the late-afternoon sun
streams onto the porch.

Exotic parrot and painted tulips are mixed with two shades of luscious lilacs. Electric chartreuse euphorbia and coral roses are the exclamation points.

Every year I look forward to the moment when my lilacs and exotic black and purple tulips bloom simultaneously.

Charles Joly lilac

Dwight D. Eisenhower lilac

Golden Fantasy rose

MY FAVORITE TULIPS ARE THE black parrot and a range of beautifully marked Rembrandt tulips that combine so well with the deep purple Charles Joly and the paler Dwight D. Eisenhower lilacs. Mixing the purple tulips and lilacs as my base color, I can make endless combinations with the soft pinks, strong reds, yellows, or whites of other flowers. In this particular bouquet I include the electric chartreuse of *Euphorbia polychroma*, the soft apricot and deep wine Lyric iris, and a few salmon roses purchased from the flower market.

LUSCIOUS LAVENDERS AND LILACS
(for bouquet on page 92)

8 stems of Dwight D. Eisenhower lilac

6 stems of Charles Joly lilac

6 mixed Rembrandt tulips

5 black parrot tulips

4 Queen of the Night tulips

12 blue parrot tulips

4 salmon roses (florist roses)

8 stems of Euphorbia polychroma

3 Lyric irises

---

1. Position the lilacs in the vase, creating a grid with their strong stems to hold the other flowers.

2. Add the remaining flowers in the following order: tulips, roses, euphorbia. Save the irises for last, since they are the most delicate.

Euphorbia polychroma

Magician tulip

Queen of the Night tulip

Mary Rose rose

Black Parrot tulip

Rembrandt tulip

Shirley tulip

Blue Parrot tulip

Iceberg rose

Mary Rose rose

For some reason, white lilacs bloom slightly longer than my lavender ones do. After the big lilac flourish subsides, I am grateful to have my white lilacs for that extra week. This special lilac combines beautifully with Iceberg (white), Heritage (light peach) and Mary Rose (pink) roses for an ideal bouquet for a June wedding.

Mme. Lemoine

These soft whites and pale

pinks make a romantic bouquet.

Porcelina

Minuette

peonies are beautiful,

Super
lilacs

Champagne

Hydrangea

fragrant, and virtually effortless to showcase.

Super flower

Icelandics

Peonies only **bloom** for three weeks but during this period my house is **filled** with their **sumptuous** beauty.

These pink peonies are beautiful, fragrant, and virtually effortless to showcase. A few flowers hurriedly stuck in several blue-and-white vases instantly transform a room.

Peonies and some of my
early pink roses are
a wonderful combination.
I always have a small
bouquet of them on
my dressing table so that
they are the first thing
that I see each morning.

WORKING WITH color was one of my favorite aspects of designing clothes, and is one of the many reasons that I adore flowers. Yet at times it is refreshing to fill my house with just white flowers. Whether that be five single-petaled peonies with their vibrant yellow centers, or a huge mass of four or five different white varieties, these flowers bring light, fragrance, and beauty into the house.

CONDITIONING TIPS

Cut peony stems on an angle and scrape the bottom 2 inches of the stem to expose the flesh.

Place the peonies in warm water containing flower preservative for a few hours and then arrange them in their final vase.

Red Grace

My favorite peony colors are the deep scarlets and magentas. This simple color combination of deep red on white makes an immediate impact on guests. The miniature ceramic flowers and the vases all come from an inexpensive shop in Venice.

I GROW SEVERAL TYPES OF peonies in Weatherstone, and every year I add new varieties as they appear on the market. I favor the deep ruby reds, scarlets, and magentas, the bluish and warm blush pinks, a variety of whites, and a few Japanese varieties (single-petaled with vibrant exotic centers) that give added texture to the more classic full-blown varieties.

1. As soon as the Klemm peony catalog arrives on my doorstep, I begin planning my peony garden. I grow lots of peonies and enjoy filling my house with them. 2. Peonies give an instantaneous burst of color and fragrance wherever they are used, and just a dozen luscious pink peonies in a blue-and-white vase bring an entire room to life. 3. Three novelty peonies cluster nicely in a simple vase. 4. Peonies allow me to be lazy. Just a handful of flowers in a vase makes a handsome bouquet. 5. The Japanese variety of tree peonies is so magnificent that one blossom makes a spectacular statement. 6. A pair of English vases look lovely with three peonies apiece.

summer

I N THE LATE SPRING I HOST A ROMANTIC GARDEN dance and use masses of peonies as my decor. In order to have the maximum number of peonies in bloom on the same date, I condition them for a full week. Some blooms I cut up to five days in advance and store in a highly air-conditioned room. Others I place in tepid water in a warm room to speed the blooms. The rest I rely on mother nature to condition.

I line inexpensive celadon pots with plastic containers holding oasis and water mixed with a flower preservative. I divide armfuls of scarlet, white, pink, and mixed peonies among the containers and parcel out the arrangements to each table.

Old French rose trellises that weren't being used in the rose garden hold terra-cotta pots of peonies and votive candles.

I want the glorious pink, red, and white peonies to provide the only color, so I set the tables with neutral taupe linens and clear glass plates, stemware, and votives. Throughout the trees I hang dozens of Japanese lanterns, and as night falls they resemble dozens of full moons swaying in the trees.

dance in june

1 2a

2b

5

4 3

1. The beginning preparation for the party. All of the bouquets for the tables were done the day before and left in a cold office with maximum air-conditioning to hold the perfect condition of the flowers until the following night. 2a and 2b. Placido and I prepare the rose trellises with containers of peonies. 3. A completed white peony table— the Japanese lanterns are lit at dusk and raised into the air, creating summer magic. 4. I tie variegated ivy with raffia bows on the backs of each chair for an additional touch. 5. We put wire platforms inside each lantern to hold the votive candles and fasten a fishing line with sinkers to each lantern.

The finished old French rose trellises display bouquets of peonies, variegated ivy, and clustered votive candles. The trellises are decorated late in the afternoon when the sun is less intense.

Pale pink peonies: Nick Shaylor, Moon River. Red and deep pink peonies: Heritage, Geny, Red Grace, Glowing Raspberry Rose. White peonies: Krinkled White, Festiva Maxima, Marshmallow Puff.

june wedding

ALWAYS LOVED DESIGNING THE BRIDAL GOWN for the end of a fashion collection. It was only natural then for me to do a bridal table when I started my "collection" of flowers. I have so often seen baby's breath misused (two sprigs stuck in with a dozen roses and some asparagus fern). I find that it is truly magical used en masse. Baby's breath is the tulle of flowers; they both give an airy fairylike quality but are easy on the wallet.

Bridal wreath (or spirea) is another flower that I enjoy using for weddings. It is a bigger bloom than baby's breath, and the two combine beautifully.

BRIDAL GARLAND

28 bunches of baby's breath

30 branches of bridal wreath

White nylon cord, white cotton string

1. To decorate the champagne table, I use a white piqué bed coverlet as the tablecloth and fasten yards of white tulle around the edges of the table with needle and thread or strips of Velcro. Fill each of the porcelain containers on top of the table with 2½ bunches of baby's breath and 10 branches of bridal wreath.

2. To make the garland, measure the amount of heavy white nylon cord needed for the base. With the cotton string, tie small handfuls of baby's breath in overlapping clusters along the length of the nylon cord. The size of your clusters depends on how wide you want the finished garland to be—in this instance 7 inches. You will need roughly 20 large bunches of baby's breath for this. Make the garland a day before the wedding and store it in damp newspaper in the cellar so that it remains moist and fresh.

Summer

Summer is truly

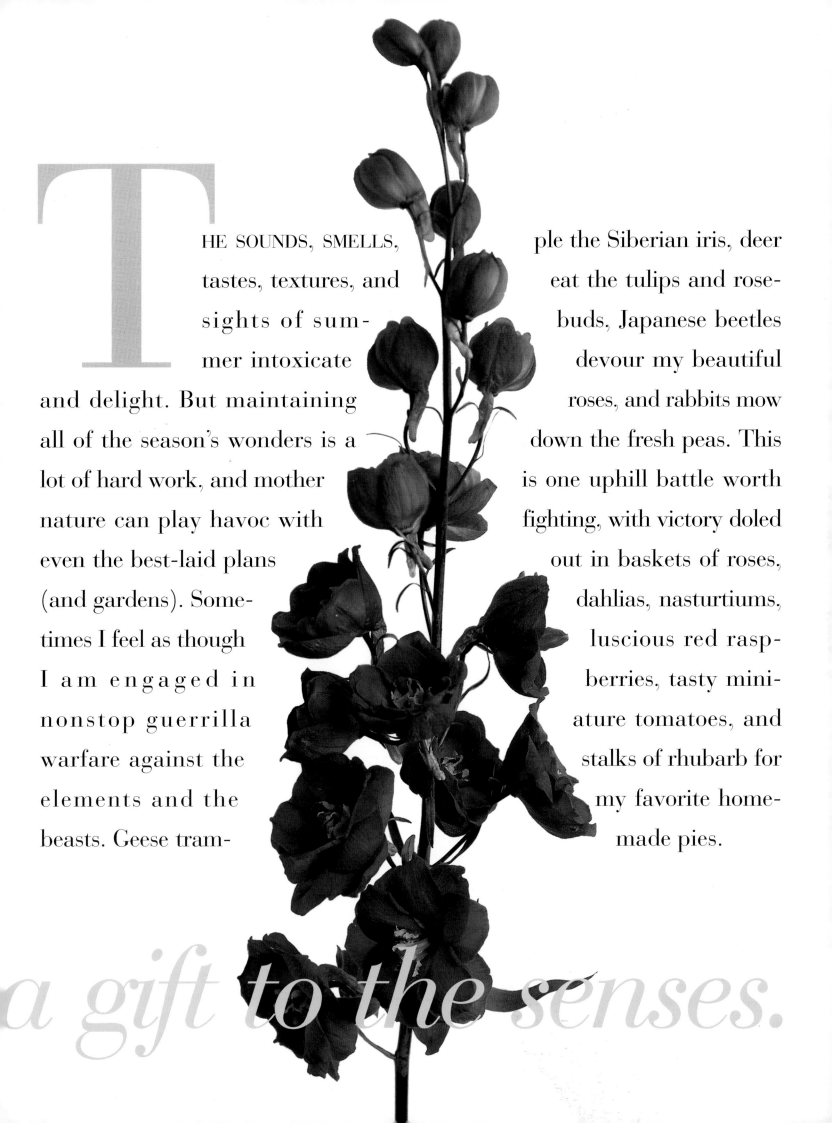

The sounds, smells, tastes, textures, and sights of summer intoxicate and delight. But maintaining all of the season's wonders is a lot of hard work, and mother nature can play havoc with even the best-laid plans (and gardens). Sometimes I feel as though I am engaged in nonstop guerrilla warfare against the elements and the beasts. Geese trample the Siberian iris, deer eat the tulips and rosebuds, Japanese beetles devour my beautiful roses, and rabbits mow down the fresh peas. This is one uphill battle worth fighting, with victory doled out in baskets of roses, dahlias, nasturtiums, luscious red raspberries, tasty miniature tomatoes, and stalks of rhubarb for my favorite homemade pies.

a gift to the senses.

bachelor's buttons

bells of ireland

clematis

coreopsis

cosmos

dahlias

delphinium

heliotrope

hollyhocks

hydrangeas

lilies

marigolds

nasturtiums

queen anne's lace

roses

rudbeckia

sunflowers

sweet peas

yarrow

zinnias

Pale blue delphiniums in an old watering can are an uncomplicated but bold accent for an area requiring a large bouquet. Any unadorned vessel such as a galvanized bucket, old sap bucket, or antique flower market container works well for this arrangement.

The Fourth of July in small-town New England still has the aura and charm of another era.

I decorate my Fourth of July table with blue linen and an inexpensive blue vase filled with early red dahlias. It is a quick and easy table setting and yet quite effective. These Burma Gem scarlet dahlias sizzle in a basic blue bowl.

The electric blues of bachelor's buttons are magnificent. For a summer picnic lunch I spread a white cotton tablecloth on the ground and fill a small tin cachepot from a local bric-a-brac fair with brilliant bachelor's buttons, bright yellow yarrow, and vivid violas.

TIN CACHEPOT

40 stems of yarrow, 70 stems of bachelor's buttons

Green florist's string, a medium-sized container,

33 single tufted pansies

Tie the yarrow into 4 bunches and the bachelor's buttons into
5 bunches with florist's string. Combine the bunches in the
container and insert 18 of the single tufted pansies throughout.
Arrange the remaining 15 pansies in a ring around the base
of the container.

SMALL TERRA-COTTA POTS

3 small nosegays of bachelor's buttons with 35 flowers apiece

*Green florist's string to better control the shape
of the clusters*

3 nosegays of yarrow Moonshine with 8 full stems apiece

Several old or used terra-cotta pots, small plastic cups

Remove the leaves and trim the stems of 35 bachelor's
buttons. Gather them into a tight, round cluster and tie them
with string. To create an equal-sized bouquet of yarrow,
bunch together approximately 8 to 10 stems and tie. Place
each bouquet in a terra-cotta pot lined with a plastic cup.

GREAT GARDENS in England and France grow towering spires of delphinium en masse. I try to imitate them, but I have resigned myself to considering this backbone of the English perennial garden as an annual in my soil. Without a more temperate climate I am constantly staking what few stalks of delphinium I have so they stand proudly in the perennial border. What I cannot harvest I purchase in the flower market. The Dutch have cultivated a variety that is magnificent in size with a less breakable stem than mine.

1. In colors from the cool part of the color spectrum are the green bells of Ireland, electric blue delphinium, and a magenta wild phlox. These flowers are interesting to look at individually or (2) blended together in a bouquet. 3. Delphinium Blue Heaven and Fire Crest sweet peas nicely reflect the colors of this old English potpourri vase. 4. Simple blue and white make a classic combination that looks beautiful in this setting. 5. From the flower market I cull big spires of delphinium, cerise ranunculus, and iridescent tulips. 6. A bucket of Queen Anne's lace and delphinium wait to be arranged.

Blue and white are easy to work with and so versatile. Great collections of delftware and pictures of beautifully tiled rooms in Portugal inspired me to decorate a blue-and-white-tiled room in my Southampton house. Every color works so well in it and the flower possibilities against this background are limitless.

Filigreed Queen Anne's lace and pristine white cosmos are as fresh as a clear summer day.

My blue-and-white collectibles represent many different styles and origins. This English Parian ware pitcher makes a charming picture filled with pristine white cosmos and Queen Anne's lace gathered from the fields behind our house.

ROSES HAVE INSPIRED POEMS, SON-nets, music, paintings, perfumes, and textiles. The rose is our national flower and the emblem of our finest feeling—love.

My first garden at Weatherstone consisted of a row of pink roses at the front of my house. For the first couple of years the garden was pretty much limited to various hybrid tea roses that I bought locally. Eventually I became somewhat more adventurous and added older varieties of roses that are now readily available in nurseries and mail-order catalogs.

Over the years I also added more rose gardens. Now in addition to my pink one I have a red garden, an apricot and yellow garden, and a white and blush garden. There is a section filled with old roses, and I planted a low hedge of ramblers that cascade into the water of an ornamental canal. The scent of the roses and the soothing quality of the water make this area one of the gems of my garden.

Like all things worthwhile, roses are not without their problems. Our vicious cold winters keep my climbers from growing large enough to scale trees or walls. And summer is spent in open warfare with the pests—primarily Japanese beetles and deer—that decimate the beautiful blooms. The battle is worth it, though, as I head out to the garden in the early morning to harvest that day's crop of roses. Color, size, shape, single-petaled or multi, scented or not—the varieties to be found in the rose world seem endless. *Right*: These various shapes and colors complement one another. A majolica pitcher filled with a mix of roses from the garden decorates the porch on a lovely June day.

the *rose* is the

The roses Sally Holmes,
Mary Rose, the Fairy,
Ambridge, Heritage,
William Shakespeare,
the Pilgrim, Sea Foam, Fair
Bianca, and Carefree
Wonder create a wonderful
summer bouquet.

most universally loved flower

English Garden

Graham Thomas

Distant Drum

I gave this old sap bucket filled with yellow, peach, apricot, and coral roses from my garden to a friend for his birthday. Most of these blooms are from my beloved bushes that horticulturist David Austin has developed.

LEFT: While huge luscious bouquets of roses are a great pleasure, a small vase with just a few blossoms can be just as beautiful and effective. I fill two small blue-and-white Wedgwood vases with 2 Graham Thomas, 3 Distant Drum, 6 English Garden.

I LOVE TO ENTERTAIN WHEN my rose gardens are in full bloom. Whether it's in the form of a large bouquet for a luncheon on the patio or a small cluster in each guest room, I allow my roses to take center stage throughout the house and garden.

Some years ago I planted a small garden of old roses. While they bloom only once in the season and perhaps are not the ideal cutting flower, their scent and color cannot be surpassed. The deep blue-red of the Tuscany and Rosa Mundi, an early variegated rose cultivated since 1521, is lovely, TOP LEFT. *Eight or nine of these delicate blossoms make an elegant bouquet.*

I feel as if I am walking through a fairyland when the walls of the garden are covered in intertwining roses and clematis. Combined here, LEFT, *are the clematis, Mrs. Cholmondely, and old roses Rosa Mundi, Comte de Chambord, and Tuscany.*

With the exception of the soft yellow rose Zitronenfalter, all of these pink roses, RIGHT, *are from my pink rose garden. Charles Rennie Macintosh, Simplicity, Gertrude Jekyll, Bell Story, Pretty Jessica, Mary Rose. To create a lovely bouquet simply combine 2 to 3 of each of these roses. Finish with 1 yellow Zitronenfalter.*

There are so many hues of any given color. The nuances of these three flowers are subtle, but they blend together as one color. OPPOSITE: These miniature reproduction blue-and-white vases are perfect for miniature bouquets at a luncheon table. The bluish pink flowers with the blue and white are fresh and feminine.

For a Large Vase:
8 pink Japanese
anemones and buds,
11 pink cosmos,
1 Mary Rose rose.
For a Small Vase:
1 pink Japanese
anemone and buds,
1 pink cosmos.

hydrangeas

and roses are splendid partners

pale blue
hydrangea

pink-and-green
hydrangea

pale green
hydrangea

Heather
rose

lavender
hydrangea

Limone
rose

Rose
Danielle

As much as I love Mop-head hydrangeas,
they do not grow well in my Connecticut soil and
climate. To satiate my appetite for them I
purchase large quantities at the market all summer
long. LEFT: These lovely pastel hydrangeas,
and a selection of florist roses in gentle hues make
a luscious and feminine bouquet.

This photograph represents a lot of favorites—blue-and-white porcelain, a dog, and flowers in blue-purple and red. One fabulous stalk of double hollyhock spices up this still life with a flash of pink.

For the Tall Vase: 1 stalk pink double hollyhock, 3 Mop-head blue hydrangeas, 3 Othello roses, 3 Rio Garnet dahlias, 16 purple and blue Pacific Giant delphinium. For the Short Vase: 13 Mop-head blue hydrangeas, 8 Red Garnet dahlias, 3 Othello roses, 10 Intrigue roses.

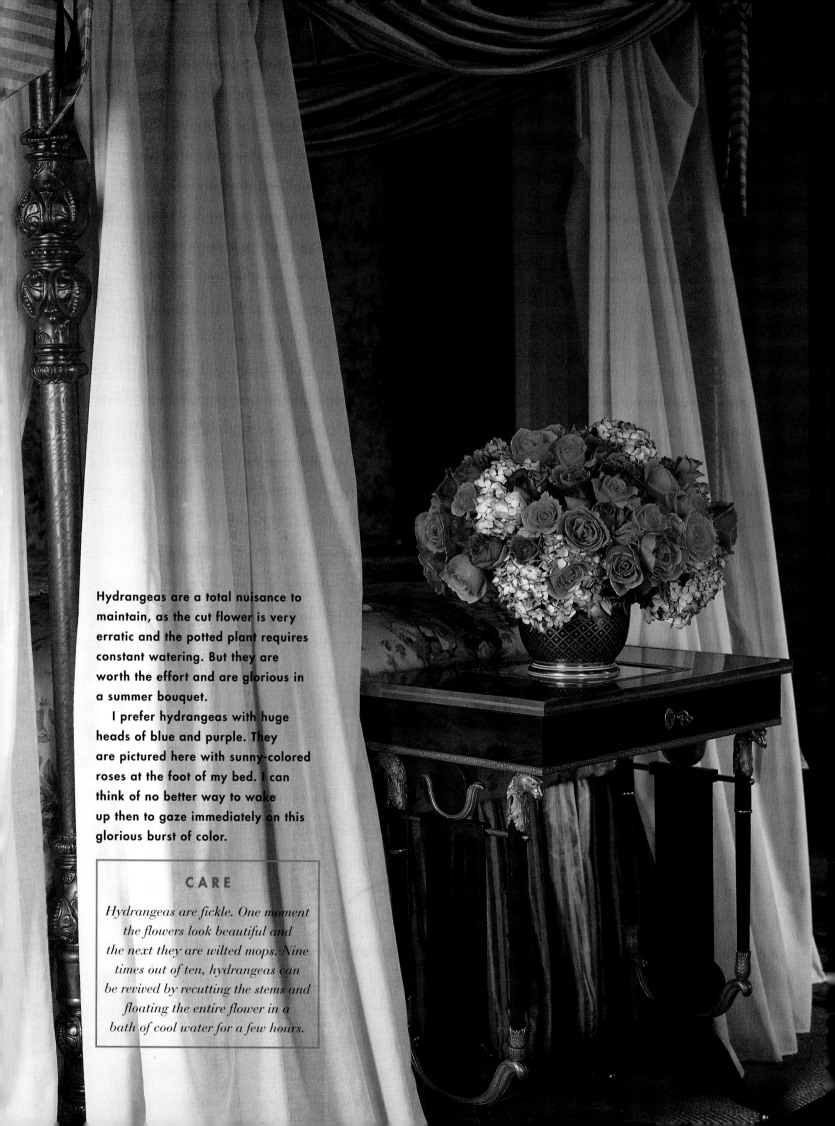

Hydrangeas are a total nuisance to maintain, as the cut flower is very erratic and the potted plant requires constant watering. But they are worth the effort and are glorious in a summer bouquet.

I prefer hydrangeas with huge heads of blue and purple. They are pictured here with sunny-colored roses at the foot of my bed. I can think of no better way to wake up then to gaze immediately on this glorious burst of color.

CARE

Hydrangeas are fickle. One moment the flowers look beautiful and the next they are wilted mops. Nine times out of ten, hydrangeas can be revived by recutting the stems and floating the entire flower in a bath of cool water for a few hours.

These soft colors work well in a large French cachepot. While this is a huge bouquet it would be just as pretty on a smaller scale. For this mix of blue hydrangeas and yellow roses: 19 Golden Fantastic roses, 21 Sensation roses, 9 Pareo roses, 13 Confetti roses, 9 blue hydrangeas.

nasturtiums

M Y GARDEN RESTS FOR TWO OR three weeks after the voluptuous July bounty subsides. Following this brief repose it bursts forth with what I call the "hot-weather, hot-color flowers."

Sunflowers, zinnias, lilies, nasturtiums, marigolds, cosmos, and glorious dahlias awaken the cutting garden in an explosion of strong color. Until the first frost the garden is truly sun-kissed.

Monet's Giverney immortalized nasturtiums by creating low borders running down the allée of the central axis for this famous garden. Another claim to fame for nasturtiums is that they are edible, as American chefs rediscovered in the 1980s. I remember eating salad after salad decorated with this flower. Personally, I prefer to look at them on my table rather than eat them, though.

Bright red-orange nasturtiums are the most common, but this flower grows in many other colors as well, including deep scarlet, coral, burnt orange, creamy white, yellow, and yellow-orange. My favorite is a beautiful striated cognac brown that I include in early-fall bouquets.

For those of us who do not have access to a beach, lunch or dinner at the pool is a wonderful way to enjoy a few hours during the summer. My poolside meals run the gamut in formality from plastic glasses and plates loaded with chips and sandwiches to more elaborate affairs.

As the colors of the
nasturtiums are so luminous
and bright—almost
hot—I keep the rest of my
table cool with shades
of green, lime, chartreuse,
and emerald.

It is rare to see an orange pansy, but I found a pot of them in the greenhouse and mixed them with a stem of yarrow to make a simple summer bouquet.

Hot-colored lilies don't blend well in my perennial garden, so I plant them in pots and scatter them about wherever I need a sunny addition. Bright yellow and orange lilies provide the inspiration for this late-summer dinner. The ochre and oranges of the majolica plates and the table linens reflect this sunny summery theme.

For a summer lunch under the trees I use deep vivid magenta and chartreuse zinnias as a lift to a very cool summer table of greens and neutrals. Granny Smith apples and green grapes look fresh and bright with these brilliantly colored flowers.

148

zinnias

Zinnias remind me of the country and summers on my grandmother's farm. She always filled her cutting garden with them.

I find big mounds of marigolds

For a poolside meal I use three different colors—French Vanilla, Orange Galore, Gold Galore—of this big fluffy marigold in squarish handmade terra-cotta pots. The rest of the table also resonates summer with hot colors (such as lemon, yellow-ochre, and orange), bamboo flatware, raffia table runners, crisp linens, and tortoiseshell glasses.

quite chic.

sunflowers

For the Large Central Vase: helianthus, 12 Prado gold, 5 sunbeam, 1 giant sun gold, 2 Fashion Mix. For the Smaller Blue Bulb Vases: 3 Prado gold, 3 sunbeam, 2 Fashion Mix, 2 buds.

I CANNOT IMAGINE A SUMMER WITHOUT THE sunny energy of sunflowers. Towering with the hollyhocks, they give architectural stature to a garden. Luckily, the sunflower has enjoyed a return to fashion in the last several years and is readily on display at every New York City greengrocer during July, August, and September, and it lasts a long time as a cut flower.

The first year I planted sunflowers I used a pretty conventional mix of bright yellows, *Helianthus valentine*, sunbeam, and Russian giant. Over the last couple of seasons I have added new varieties that are more varied in color such as Burpees Fashion Mix, Velvet Queen, a rich brown, and Prado red.

More traditional sunflowers are bold and colorful blended in cobalt blue glass containers. Mixed with blue cut crystal, painted Sienese plates, and a blue-and-white-striped tablecloth, they produce a great-looking summer table.

Overleaf: I have added new and more sophisticated colorings of sunflowers to the garden as I come across them. Deep velvety brown and rich russet colors are alluring against a neutral table setting. Wooden-handled flatware, a straw runner, basket-encased glasses, English drabware plates, and beige linen napkins tied with a strand or two of raffia make a summery background for these exotic flowers.

For a large bouquet of velvety brown sunflowers: 17 Fashion Mix, 4 Velvet Queen, 1 Prado Red.

156

1. These miniature sunflowers are a great way to decorate a breakfast tray or a small nook. 2. A handful of sunflowers decorates an afternoon tea tray nicely. 3. A large blue majolica pitcher of *Rudbeckia tribola* makes a colorful summer bouquet. 4. Sunflowers (in water pics) nestle among lemons and limes to create a great summer centerpiece.

Envy

Fire Magic

Gold
Kist

Marmalade

Neon
Splendor

Sugar Cane

dahlias

Red Garnet

Rip City

Fascination

Ali Oop

Burma Gem

I have collected majolica vases, plates, and pitchers for the last fifteen years and I find these small pitchers perfect containers for bright summery flowers. For summer luncheons or dinner I often put a large pitcher of mixed flowers in the center of the table and arrange individual bouquets for each place setting.

gold galore marigold

heliotrope

assorted pansies

rudbeckia tribola

glorious daisy

pink cosmos

sedum autumn joy

purple tesanthus

assorted nasturtiums

ZINNIAS

silver sun (soft green)

envy
(strong chartreuse)

crimson monarch
(deep red)

cherry sun
(a medium pinkish-red)

scarlet splendor
(scarlet)

DAHLIAS

swans desert storm

chembino

awaikoe

arabian night

gitt's respect

I RESERVE THE LARGEST amount of room in my cutting gardens for dahlias. From the first blooms in July to the last in October (provided we don't have an early frost), they brighten my home, decorate tables, and overflow from my garden. I have some varieties that are the size of small dinner plates—needless to say, one blossom is a bouquet. Dahlias come in a range of colors from oranges, apricots, corals, and reds and whites to exotic purples and bordeaux. My favorites are the deep rich burgundies and purples highlighted with the two-toned white and purple-edged dahlias such as Ryan. They are beautiful by themselves or mixed with other flowers and berries.

As we get into late September I begin checking the weather report. One shot of frost will wipe out the whole dahlia crop, so as soon as I get the first warning I race to the garden and bundle them up for one last burst of magical color indoors.

Dahlias explode from this reproduction Chinese footbath. The colors are exhilarating and they fill the house with sunshine.

I enjoy this arrangement as a transition from late summer to early fall. The luscious peaches of August and the first autumnal touch of viburnum berries in reds and yellows mix beautifully with these exotic two-toned Orange Julius and Gitt's Respect dahlias in my favorite majolica pitcher.

Autumn

last loveliest smile.

—*William Cullen Bryant*

T

HERE IS NO PLACE more beautiful in autumn than New England. We revel in the amazing colors, the sound of rustling leaves, and the smell of wood smoke from the first fires of the season. Sugar maples line the road with intense reds and golds, the apple orchards burst with fruit, and squashes, gourds, and pumpkins ripen in the garden. I use seasonal flowers, leaves, and berries throughout the house, making my home a display of autumn beauty. Cozy chats in front of the fire, football games and tailgates, pies bubbling in the oven, the occasional square-dance, Halloween parties, and lots of laughter fill the air.

Autumn, the year's

apples

asters

bittersweet

chocolate cosmos

chrysanthemums

dahlias

gourds

hypernicum

maple leaves

pumpkins

rose hips

roses

skimmia

smoke bush

snowberries

squash

viburnum berries

wild blackberries

Showbiz
rose

Mon Cheri rose

Red Garnet
dahlia

Antonia
Ridge rose

viburnum

Arabian
Night dahlia

autumn

Bright red dahlias and roses fill the room with their intensity. Viburnum berries provide a blast of vibrant color while their prettily shaped leaves create a border around the flowers and berries.

For this bouquet I fill a lined basket with 8 stems viburnum, 3 Red Garnet and 2 Arabian Night dahlias, 5 Antonia Ridge, 11 Showbiz, and 3 Mon Cheri roses.

dahlias

Mystique dahlia

sedum

wild blackberry

chocolate cosmos

OPPOSITE: Within this antique green glass match striker, wild blackberries and sedum give a wonderful texture to a small bouquet of dahlias and chocolate cosmos. The small velvety chocolate cosmos are one of my favorite flowers to use in fall arrangements—and they even smell like chocolate.

For this bouquet I used 6 chocolate cosmos, 5 Arabian Night dahlias, 8 Mystique dahlias, 8 small heads of sedum, 3 stems Autumn Joy wild blackberry (in bud).

More than anything I must have

flowers always, always.
—Claude Monet

Dahlias of brilliant red and rich maroons mix with blackberries and roses in this simple tarnished brass vase. A salver of concord and champagne grapes complete the autumn table. For this arrangement I use 8 Rip City, 12 Fire Magic, 2 Zorro, and 2 Arabian Night dahlias, 1 Ingrid Bergman rose, and 8 stems wild blackberries.

Bread feeds the body indeed, but flowers feed also the soul.
—The Koran

SHADES OF BROWN and white make a chic and tailored theme for an early fall luncheon. These horn-and-silver containers look great but do not hold water. Each one must be lined with a heavy plastic bag and stuffed with a small piece of oasis to give it weight and to anchor the dahlia stems.

LARGE CONTAINER

3 Brookside Snowball dahlias

5 white L'Ancresso dahlias

1 dahlia bud

BEAKERS

4 Brookside Snowball dahlias

1. The soft mauves of anemonies, Ryan and Burma Gem dahlias, and chocolate cosmos fill this small majolica pitcher. 2. A small nineteenth-century English vase of bright yellow-orange and red dahlias mixed with a handful of the last nasturtiums from the garden. 3. A silver pitcher of some of my favorite dahlias— Patches, Rip City, Winter Ice, Fascination, Fire Magic, and Touch of Class—rests prettily on this corner table. 4. Chocolate cosmos, Showbiz spray roses, Arabian Night and Red Garnet dahlias, and a few deep purple basil leaves combine beautifully in this small Russian vase. 5. A large cachepot holds purple-hued dahlia, teal-violet and garnet hydrangeas, and poppy pods. 6. A variety of white dahlias consort with snowberry branches.

CHRYSANTHEMUMS evoke memories of homecoming weekends, bonfires, parades, and corsages tied with ribbons in the school colors. Their form is beautiful and luscious, and they thrive when the rest of my garden is on its last leg. I put big terra-cotta pots filled with russet Bordeaux and yellow chrysanthemums throughout the house and on the porch where we enjoy the last warm days of the year.

RIGHT: Willow baskets provide a simple rustic background for these classic California chrysanthemums.

chrysanthemum

This often maligned flower is truly elegant and the essence of autumn.

A ball of russet chrysanthemum pompons makes a
chic bouquet in this wooden
pedestal vase. Since the
container is porous, I line it
with a plastic Tupperware
container filled with a block
of oasis.

Every flower about a house certifies to

Whether arranged in elegant
Japanese bronze vases or
in a pair of inexpensive willow
baskets, these California
mums are chic and endure
well as a cut flower.
The tall vase holds 22 of
these yellow mums
while the short vase
contains 6.

the refinement of somebody.

—Robert G. Ingersoll

In the country I fill large lined baskets with vivid chrysanthemums in a range of colors. Shots of magenta sparkle amidst the oranges, yellows, and rusts.

TOP: A small English pitcher is filled with yarrow and daisy-shaped chrysanthemums.

Autumn-toned yarrow, skimmia, asters, chrysanthemums, sedum, viburnum berries, and nonflowering seed pods pick up the colors in the small pitchers they fill.

Asters are the other staple of the fall floral community. Whether it is the small daisylike aster, or the larger pompon variety, asters are colorful, gay, and a great autumn accent for any room.

These magenta and purple asters in a wooden basket spruce up an entranceway.

Vividly colored *asters*

echo the bright foliage in New England.

berries. A mix of rose hips and
the last nasturtiums of the
season fill the ice bucket on the
left. In the middle vase rests a
bouquet of fresh yellow
bittersweet, rose hips, and
hypernicum berries. The last
oak beaker brims with more
young bittersweet, golden
dahlias, and nasturtiums.

russet, golden yellow, amber,

ochre, and bittersweet orange

I still carve pumpkins for Halloween. My jack-o'-lantern faces are always very simple, but they give a happy (never sinister) face to a Halloween night buffet table. A simple arrangement of hay, fall leaves, votive candles, and pumpkins provide a nest for the pumpkin pie, Halloween cookies, apple crisp, and baked apples for the dessert table.

Spring blossoms mature into

the fall where we dine under

baskets of apples in
the **fruit**-laden trees.

A S THE DAYS become shorter I dine outside as often as possible. In the orchard I prepare an alfresco pre-harvest lunch under the trees, and set the rustic table with blue-and-white transfer-print china and simple hand-stitched napkins. In the middle of the table rests a pumpkin with a crown of bittersweet and trails of apples.

199

It is usually warm enough on Halloween to have a lunch on the porch. I dress the table in earth tones in keeping with an autumn setting. Strands of raffia with twigs of bittersweet adorn the orange linens, terra-cotta baskets, and the large basket filled with gourds and miniature pumpkins from the garden. Clusters of rose hips vary the texture on the table and complement the ochre ceramic dishes.

I cherish these last outdoor lunches on the

final warm golden days of fall.

HALLOWEEN LUNCHEON TABLE

Assorted bittersweet vines

5 sprigs rose hips

Raffia

Plastic liner

*5 sprigs small
yellow chrysanthemums*

*7 medium-sized
russet chrysanthemums*

1. Measure the size of your container and make a closed garland of bittersweet to fit. In this case I bend single vines around the basket and attach them to the handles. Tie clusters of rose hips to the bittersweet with raffia. Line the terra-cotta container with plastic and fill with a mixture of chrysanthemums, and more rose hips.

2. Overlap long strands of bittersweet that have not been deleafed along the handle and perimeter of the basket and fasten with raffia.

3. To continue the theme I tie raffia with a sprig of bittersweet around burnt orange linen napkins.

4. The finished table combines textures and fruits from an autumn garden for a lovely fall luncheon.

bittersweet, squash,

I enjoy hosting a big party in the fall featuring a square dance. Naturally, the food and decor reflect the folksy autumn ambience. Bittersweet, squash, pumpkins, pears, fallen leaves, and ochre candles scatter along the table in a pretty fall glow.

pumpkins, fallen leaves

Russet, rust, deep orange, warm red, and peach roses coordinate beautifully with autumn fruits, berries, and leaves. LEFT: A bronze doré cachepot and rustic terra-cotta pitcher brim with autumn roses and rose hips. Both arrangements reflect the warmth and charm of autumn.

Fall colors in a rust-colored antique Chinese bud vase highlight this Leon Otis rose with contrasting vibrant inner petals and pale buff outer ones.

A pair of Russian memorial cups from the era of Nicholas II, OPPOSITE, filled with small peach and burnt orange roses create a warm tableau.

The cornucopia of fruit is a classic symbol of Thanksgiving bounty. Here I fill an English wine cooler with fruits that reflect the seventeenth-century painting behind it. It does not matter what style the environment is, but all the elements should enhance one another.

"In everything give thanks."
—*Thessalonians*

THERE ARE MANY WAYS OF CELEBRATing Thanksgiving, including large buffets for friends and family, intimate formal dinners, and large country lunches. My menu is basically uniform, but I create small variations congruous with the surrounding environment and guests. For example, I serve small individual pumpkin pies for a buffet, pumpkin soufflé for a more formal dinner, and a deep-dish lattice-top pumpkin pie and turkey-shaped sugar cookies for an informal country lunch. My flowers also reflect these changes in style.

A large flat basket filled with apples, grapes, black viburnum berries, and skimmia creates a rustic centerpiece. Individual baskets with skimmia and viburnum look charming and hold the place cards.

Overleaf: For a small, elegant Thanksgiving dinner I combine gold table accessories with The Statesman gold button chrysanthemums. These flowers are rich, beautiful, affordable, and versatile. I have also used these vibrant flowers just as effectively in a simple rustic basket for a dinner in the country.

thanksgiving

For my city buffet I fill my favorite silver tureen with a mass of glorious roses, burgundy astilbe, skimmia, and the maroon leaves of smoke bush to create the richly colored and textured centerpiece. This is a very large bouquet, but naturally, it can be done on any scale.

THANKSGIVING LUNCH IN THE COUNTRY

5 small containers

3½ dozen small, dark red apples

10 stems skimmia

8 stems viburnum berries

Sticky cling

7 small clusters of red grapes

1. Place small containers sporadically throughout a bottom layer of apples to provide water for the skimmia and viburnum berries. Attach the containers to the basket with sticky cling (a gummy florist's clay) so they do not move around.

2. Tie bunches of skimmia and berries and place them in the containers of water.

3. Arrange apples and grapes around the flower clusters

4. Attach the last apples and grapes to one another with sticky cling to keep the centerpiece together.

CITY BUFFET

18 branches smoke bush

2 dozen stems skimmia

2 dozen burgundy Astilbe

1½ dozen red velvet roses

1½ dozen Golden Sensation roses

1½ dozen orange dahlias

1. Place a ball of chicken wire in your container and arrange the smoke bush branches as a framework for your more delicate flowers. Surround with a border of skimmia (since these have shorter stems they tend to work better along the lip of the container for this arrangement).

2. Weave in Astilbe.

3. Continue to fill in the arrangement with Astilbe until it is rather full. Poke in the roses and dahlias.

4. The finished arrangement works well in a variety of containers, including a rustic basket or fancy silver tureen.

Winter

Winter covers the world

T HE FIRST SNOW-fall of the season is as exciting as the first crocus surfacing at the end of winter. Under cover of snow, the garden landscape takes on a sculptural guise. Like most gardeners and flower lovers, I spend the winter months poring over my gardening books and magazines and navigating the seed catalogs. I satisfy my green thumb by forcing bulbs and branches and growing spring flowers in the greenhouse. Fortunately, there are now reliable sources for beautiful flowers all year long. A nosegay of violets or a glorious bunch of daffodils brightens a room on a cold winter day and is all the more appreciated because of its seasonal rarity.

in crystal white magic.

african violets

amaryllis

bavardia

begonias

boxwood

camellias

carnations

christmas greens

clementines

eucalyptus

gardenias

hydrangeas

hypernicum

ilex berries

lady apples

large red apples

lisianthus

magnolia leaves

mini pineapples

muscari

paperwhites

pinecones

potted crocus

potted miniature daffodils

primrose

ranunculus

roses

seckel pears

skimmia

stock

tulips

variegated euphorbia
leaves

Decorating my home for
the holidays is one of the
great pleasures of my life.
This arrangement requires
a lot of roses, but it truly
transforms a room.

christmas

WHEN I WAS DESIGNING CLOTHES on Seventh Avenue, I ultimately thought of Christmas as a chore. I felt drained of energy for the whole month of December, and no matter how hard I worked, there was always more to do. A couple of years ago I began reassessing what was important to me and how to recapture the "true Christmas spirit." I simplified traditions that are dear to me and pared down a lot of the extras that weren't worth the hassle. I also discovered the joy of donating my time and creativity—not just my money —to worthy organizations. The reward has been a return to the true Christmas spirit of peace on earth and goodwill toward all.

Christmas is such an exciting time of year. The days and nights of December are filled with gazing at glimmering store windows, wrapping packages, baking cookies, singing Christmas carols, gathering at parties, praying for snow, sending cards, shopping with the crowds, buying the Christmas tree and greenery, sipping eggnog, hanging sparkling decorations, going to Christmas Eve mass, and enjoying family and friends. Christmas gives us all a chance to invite and share.

THE TEXTURE AND SCALE OF THESE flowers in varying shades of red create an intriguing bouquet. The shiny ilex berries counterpoint the matte texture of the other flowers. If available, the deeper red amaryllis (not the traditional Christmas red) adds depth to the bouquet.

When using a certain flower such as the rose, I try to find a miniature version of that rose to provide a richer texture. In this bouquet I use the small spray rose Mercedes and the larger rose Forever, for this effect.

LARGE ROUND VASE

26 Chinese Red carnations

22 Harvard Red carnations

6 stems amaryllis (with 2 to 3 blossoms per stem)

14 Mercedes roses (about 6 stems—
this is a spray rose with multiple flowers on each stem)

14 Forever roses

12 Sasha roses

12 branches ilex

1. Place all of the carnations in the vase.

2. Strategically insert the amaryllis where they will provide the strongest focal point for the bouquet.

3. Next, add the three varieties of roses.

4. Slip the shinny ilex between the velvety flowers.

There is material enough in a single flower for the **ornament** of a score of cathedrals. —*John Ruskin*

The varying sizes and colors of red within the carnations and roses create an interesting texture in this bouquet. The deep richness of the rose Black Magic, the velvety reds of the famous Red Velvet rose and the spray rose Mercedes resemble shadows and light throughout the arrangement.

To help alleviate some of the expense associated with a bouquet of this size, I have used the carnation Harvard Red as my foundation flower. The picot edge of the carnation provides additional texture.

Black Magic rose

CHRISTMAS REDS AND ROSES
(for bouquet on preceding page)

48 Red Velvet roses

34 Black Magic roses

15 stems Mercedes spray roses

52 Harvard Red carnations

1. Clean the roses and remove the leaves.

2. Cut all the flowers to a height that works proportionately with your container.

3. Insert a wedge of oasis that has been soaked in a solution of floral preservative and water.

4. Place your background flower, the Harvard Red carnations, in the container.

5. Insert small clusters of the same roses throughout the carnations. This might look off balance at first, but it will create a more alive and interesting arrangement in the end.

It is by believing in roses that one brings them to bloom.

—French proverb

For a festive look in individual cups: 3 Black Magic roses, 5 Forever Yours roses, 6 stems Mercedes spray roses, 6 branches skimmia, 5 gold poppy pods.

CENTERPIECE
(overleaf)

2 dozen red pears

*10 small pomegranates,
sprayed antique gold*

*4 miniature pineapples,
sprayed antique gold*

*2 dozen walnuts,
sprayed antique gold*

*6 sprays of an exotic nut,
sprayed antique gold*

*1½ dozen poppy pods,
sprayed antique gold*

Cling adhesive

*12 branches of skimmia,
sprayed with a glitterlike substance
from a florist supply house*

1. Stuff the bottom of the container with newspaper. This will save money and prevent the container from getting too heavy and bruising the tabletop.

2. Arrange the fruit and nuts in a pleasing pattern. Use a sticky clay substance called Cling to anchor the final pieces, as they will invariably fall off otherwise.

3. Last, insert the skimmia in water pics and strategically tuck them throughout the centerpiece.

M Y MEALS IN Connecticut range in formality from spaghetti on a tray in front of the TV to a big summer dance outdoors. In Manhattan I host my more "grown-up affairs." For this Christmas dinner for ten, I use a gold and deep garnet red theme to complement this wonderful antique dinner service. A brass English wine cooler filled with garnet-colored pears and golden fruits, nuts, and branches of skimmia serves as a festive centerpiece. To complete the table I encircle the centerpiece with gold cups filled with small nosegays of glittering roses and skimmia.

SOMETIMES I USE FLOWERS AS ACCENTS for other elements of a table or room that I want to highlight. In this case, the flowers and fruits are secondary to the tableware. This antique English service with its latticeware baskets and handsome cream soup tureen rests beautifully on a tapestry tablecloth made from a fabric remnant. To give the setting a holiday flavor I choose fruits that are traditionally found at Christmas—tiny clementines, Seckel pears, and lady apples—and blend them with russet-colored roses, skimmia, and hypernicum.

CHRISTMAS IN RUSSET TONES

12 clementines (tangerines can be substituted)

6 Seckel pears, 3 small stems lemon leaves

Cling (sticky florist's clay) or a glue gun

14 Estrella roses

5 stems skimmia (if the spray has multiple stems, break them apart so they don't overpower the roses)

8 small branches hypernicum

---

1. Pile the fruit into the container and secure any unstable pieces and the lemon leaves with Cling or a glue gun.
2. Insert roses, skimmia, and hypernicum into water vials and place within the arrangement. Two to three stems can be inserted into each vial.

THE POOR CAR-nation has such a tarnished image as a cheap flower plagued by ghastly and unnatural dye jobs. But there are an array of carnations that are beautiful and seldom seen. The fragrance of true carnations—especially those from France and Italy—is scrump-tious. Carnations, if nothing else, should appeal to our pragmatic side. They are inexpensive, avail-able almost everywhere, and more durable than just about any other flower in the market.

At Christmastime, when there is so much to do, I often pull out my Regency crystal vases and fill them with carnations. The arrangement requires no care other than fresh water, and it will last for a good ten to twelve days and free you to do a myriad of other Christmas activities.

carnations

While it is a relatively subtle difference, the use of two shades of red in this mass makes it more interesting. The Chinese Red with its orange tone is the highlight to the more sophisticated bluish red of the Harvard Red carnation. Each vase contains 32 Chinese Red carnations and 32 Harvard Red carnations.

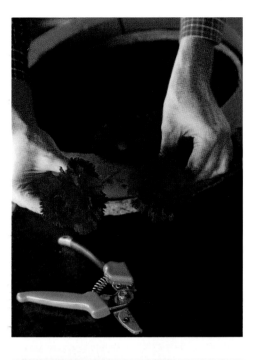

M Y CHRISTMAS wreath is the one extravagant carnation project that I indulge in—but it is extravagant in time only. Every evening I mist the carnations with water, (removing the bow which I place with a separate wire hook) and leave them in a cool place for the night. The effort is small in comparison with the impact of those beautiful reds on the wall, and the wreath can last up to twelve days.

CARNATION WREATH

Wreath ring of oasis

60 Harvard Red carnations

60 Classic Red carnations

1. Soak the oasis in water mixed with a flower preservative and let it drain.
2. Cut the stems of the carnations to 2½ inches and begin inserting them into the wreath. Alternate the two colors of carnations in an uneven pattern to keep it from looking dotted or static.
3. Let the wreath drain for an hour in a sink—otherwise it will drain on your wall.
4. Make a colored ribbon bow and hang. I use a deep iridescent forest green.

T HE SMELL OF Christmas boughs evokes many childhood memories. My mother, my grandmother, and I always decorated the house from top to bottom, and one of our favorite effects was draping generous garlands filled with pinecones over mantles and doorways and sprinkling them with a generous snowfall.

For the Weatherstone Christmas open house, I decorate a big cocktail table in the stable with baskets full of balsam, carefully placed pinecones, and a mist of artificial snow. To help anchor the pine branches I insert them into big chunks of heavy oasis or a ball of chicken wire. The pinecones are large enough to rest on top without the use of wire.

evergreen

To add shimmer I spray pinecones with antique gold paint
and wire them to the wreaths
surrounding a pair of Regency
mirrors and the apple kettle.
As a rather simple alternative
to flowers, I pile apples into a
huge bronze kettle (any large
container is effective) and
surround them with a garland
made of two types of pine and
magnolia branches, OPPOSITE.

MAGNOLIA LEAVES—WITH THEIR lacquered green surface and suedelike russet underside— make a beautiful and elegant statement on an entry table. These chic branches are quite affordable, last a long time, and do not conflict with other flowers in the house. Because of their size and architectural structure they make a bold statement when a large bouquet is needed.

During the apple harvest season of late October through Christmas I have big baskets of apples throughout my home, *previous page*. (The dogs also enjoy this tradition and happily steal from the baskets at every opportunity.) The scents of apple and pine permeate the house in a festive combination.

GARLAND
(pages 242 and 243)

Antique gold spray paint (found in craft stores)

4½ dozen pinecones of varying sizes

White pine, spruce, magnolia leaves,

Green florist's wire

Spray paint the pinecones and allow them to dry. The wreaths surrounding the mirrors and kettle are formed on a wire. An easier and faster alternative is to buy a premade garland of white pine and add another variety of pine and magnolia leaves to it with green florist's wire. Attach the pine cones with a glue gun or a piece of wire.

BRONZE KETTLE
(page 242)

4 dozen apples (more or less depending on container size)

To avoid weight and expense, I crumple newspaper at the bottom of the kettle and fill in with apples. Finish with a garland wrapped around the outer rim of the container.

winter

whites

D
URING THE HOL-
idays I sometimes feel the need to escape the reds, greens, lady apples, pomegranates, and pine-cones. This table setting of snowy whites and light blue is the perfect retreat. It is very cool, formal, and rather wintry-looking with the simple crystal, stark white linen, and blue-and-white porcelain.

Texture, scale, and variety make this blend of white hues interesting. A large amaryllis, medium-sized roses, lisianthus, carnations, smaller narcissus, bavardia, stock, and miniature carnations contrive a pleasing texture of whites. The soft sage green eucalyptus and variegated euphorbia give a sense of movement to the arrangement.

I prefer quiet New Year's Eve dinners with a few friends to large extravaganzas with throngs of partygoers. Together we reflect on the past year and discuss our hopes and aspirations for the coming one.

New Year's Eve is a night

For a change I host dinner
in my greenhouse, where
jasmine and flowering
camellias scent the air. Silver,
blue, and white provide a
bold and welcome contrast to
the Christmas reds and
greens of the preceding week.

for reflection and anticipation.

Blue and white is the
eternal color combination.

White Garden rose

AFTER THE BUSTLE OF CHRISTMAS, it is somewhat of a relief to finally pack away the decorations and break from the red, green, and gold for a while. In January and February I begin to long for the spring color palette again. I frequent flower markets and purchase pots of blooming hyacinths, tulips, daffodils, crocus, primrose, gardenias, orchids, and hydrangeas to brighten the gray winter days.

ANTIQUE BULB VASES
(opposite, from left)

5 stems paperwhites surrounded by lemon leaves

4 White Garden roses from the greenhouse

4 stems lisianthus (several blossoms per stem)

CENTER BOUQUET
(page 246)

39 white carnations

7 miniature white carnations

6 white stock

12 stems eucalyptus with berries

4 stems amaryllis

12 white roses

6 lisianthus

6 stems variegated euphorbia

5 clusters bavardia

5 clusters white narcissus

END BOUQUET
(page 246)

10 white carnations

4 miniature white carnations

6 white stock

7 stems eucalyptus with berries

2 stems amaryllis (with two to five blossoms on each stem)

5 white roses

5 lisianthus

5 stems variegated euphorbia

4 clusters bavardia

4 clusters narcissus

1. Select a large, shallow container and insert a piece of oasis as an anchor.
2. Insert the carnations, stock, and eucalyptus as the base structure of the bouquet.
3. Place the amaryllis next.
4. Add the more delicate roses, lisianthus, variegated euphorbia, and bavardia.
5. Finish with the very delicate narcissus, so they tremble just slightly above the rest of the flowers.

To create a lovely bouquet of variegated flowers in reds and yellows, combine 6 parrot tulips, 10 Sensation roses, 7 Golden Fantastic roses, 11 Confetti roses, 7 Pareo roses, 4 stems of spray roses, 6 Estrella roses, 4 sprigs of hypernicum.

Variegated flowers are mother nature's way of saying "All right, enough beauty, let's kick up our heels, create, and have fun!"

This extravagant bronze doré cachepot holds masses of variegated roses. This bouquet also works well in several smaller containers clustered or scattered around the room. Here I've used 11 Sensation roses, 15 Confetti roses, 12 Pareo roses, 6 stems of spray roses, 7 buds from the spray roses, 8 Red Velvet roses, 9 orange-red roses and 18 Forever Yours roses. Make sure to break up each color so that the end result doesn't appear spotty.

VARIEGATED flowers seem magical and work so well in holiday bouquets. In mid-December, parrot tulips start to arrive in the market. They are not as easy to find as the more traditional tulips, but they are worth the hunt.

My apartment in New York is dominated by vivid yellow walls and russet taffeta curtains. I love to use palettes of red, yellow, and soft orange in the fall and winter to give everything a cozy, golden glow. The mixture of the two-toned Rembrandt tulips, Confetti roses, charming spray roses, and hypernicum creates a series of bright patterns and textures.

Sensation rose

Confetti rose

parrot tulip

Golden Fantastic rose

hypernicum

PARIS IN THE WIN-
ter is lovely. The
gray skies make
a beautiful foil
for every color
and blend with the neutrals in
those glorious buildings. On the
other hand, choices in flower
colors are enormous, and I fill my
apartment with them.

When flowers are not readily
available or are very expensive, I
substitute flowering plants. They
add a great deal to the spirit of
my home, last a long time, and
are much less expensive than cut
flowers. Ivy, herb, and boxwood
topiaries, gardenias, orchids,
gloxinia, cyclamen, ferns, African
violets, and azaleas do well during this fallow season.

flowering

When I found these
wonderful gardenias I
planted them in my
French porcelain de Paris
ceramic baskets and
then tucked them in with
fresh moss.

plants

Carnations are fantastic flowers—their color, their form, and their scent make them so.

Flowering rose plants are very popular among many good Parisian florists. The bushes bloom for several weeks and create a lovely still life when nestled with cut flowers around them.

Roses and carnations look so pretty together. They last a long time and the carnations help reduce the cost of the arrangements.

Grape hyacinth and these
novelty miniature roses from
South Africa make a sweet
nosegay in a bedroom. Both
come packed in water and tied
into bunches ready to be
dropped into these small
Worcester porcelain vases from
antique fairs and flea markets.

fill baskets with
African violets—and
miniature violets
when I can find them.
They are so pretty
on a breakfast tray,
on a dressing table,
or placed next to the
bathroom sink.

1. Primroses seem to take away some of the chill of winter. I insert seven pots of colored primroses in my English wine cooler and tuck moss around the edges. They will bloom for three to four weeks with vigilant watering. 2. Another reliable flowering plant is the begonia. These pretty pinks and corals offer several weeks of color and look lovely in these reproduction blue-and-white containers. 3. A favorite color combination of mine is blue and chartreuse. Blue hydrangea plants in a silver soup terrine sit next to a salver of luscious green grapes. 4. Delicate purple-and-white-striped crocus hints of spring around the corner. Just two pots of them with a blanket of green moss provide a breath of fresh air. 5. This basket of primroses amid sprouts of grass makes a lovely birthday present. I line the basket with plastic before inserting the potted primroses. I encase tufts of grass in plastic bags (to keep them moist) and cover the base of the primroses in a miniature garden. Fluff the grass so it covers the edges of all the pots. 6. Miniature daffodils brighten any corner of the house. A small pot or basket bolsters everyone's spirits.

Ivy topiaries are another long-lasting option for decorating your house. I buy them from the flower market or local florist, blanket them with moss, water, and enjoy. With no fuss or bother they look great.

TOPIARY IS THE ART OF TRAINING OR cutting trees, shrubs, or other plants into interesting shapes. I've always used lots of boxwood at Christmas, but recently I began using it throughout the year. I find them so refreshing that occasionally I fill my home with just boxwood topiaries and fresh fruits such as lemons, oranges, or Granny Smith apples mixed with green grapes. The only problem is that after a short time my decor looks rather sad, as everyone passing by plucks a grape or two.

Boxwood topiaries take a bit of practice and a lot of patience, but otherwise they are easy to make and they last quite a while. Begin by soaking the boxwood branches for a day or so in tepid water. To make a round ball, *top*, carve a large block of oasis into a ball shape on top with a tree trunk stem on the bottom which will slip into a vase. Place it in a container already filled with water. Insert small branches of boxwood into the oasis to form a nice rounded shape. Trim the boxwood into a well-formed ball. If you make a mistake simply repatch the spot with fresh boxwood and begin again.

A still life of green apples, grapes, and lemon leaves and a neatly trimmed boxwood topiary will last a very long time.

Today herbal topiaries are very popular. Rather than use the traditional terra-cotta pots I place a pair of myrtle ball topiaries in small English vases and cover their bases with moss. I also "plant" some leftover grass in a third vase to create a small garden.

V

IOLETS DO NOT last long, but for their short duration they are glorious. They are so romantic that I often include them in my Valentine's Day decor. If they were more readily available as cut flowers in the states, I would encourage every man to forgo the traditional red roses and send a cluster of these enchanting flowers instead.

HEART

3 bunches violets (already tied)
Oasis (carved in a heart shape)

1. Submerge the violets in cool water for half an hour and remove.

2. Two round nosegays create the top of the heart. The third requires careful pruning to create the point of the heart.

3. Reshape the three bunches of violets so that they form a heart shape.

3. Insert the three bunches carefully into a water-soaked oasis heart.

4. Wrap the bottom of the oasis in plastic to hold the water and keep it from dripping.

valentine's

day

W HAT COULD BE more perfect for Valentine's Day than a table aglow with cranberry-colored glass? Small bouquets of Matisse roses and variegated euphorbia decorate each place setting. Each vase contains only eight to ten flowers, but with six vases arranged on the table, these scented red-and-white roses make a big impact.

WHEN ENTERTAINING ON Valentine's Day, I enjoy making individual heart-shaped bouquets for each of my guests. They are easy to do and look lovely in a guest room or holding a place-card during dinner. For each bouquet you'll need a foundation of oasis that has been cut out with a heart-shaped cookie cutter (approximately 3 to 4 inches in size and 1½ inches deep). Soak the oasis in water and wrap the bottom in plastic wrap. One bouquet requires approximately 20 roses (I use Matisse roses here) that have been cut so their stems are 1 inch long. Poke the roses into the oasis close together to cover the heart-shape and fill in with variegated euphorbia for an extra touch of color.

Right: Red and white, the obvious choices, make a romantic table. White ceramic dishes and a small cupid vase on a red damask tablecloth are the perfect background for a Valentine topiary of red-and-white tulips, variegated and solid carnations, red roses, and trailing ivy vines.

ORCED BRANCHES ARE
such a lovely harbinger of spring.
These beautiful quince blossoms
and a new coral carnation were
purchased at a market. They contribute to a very pretty winter luncheon table when mixed with some
cranberry antique glass. Despite
the cold February weather outside,
the umbrella of blossoms reminds
me of an orchard in spring. An
added benefit to this arrangement is that carnations and quince
blossoms both last a long time.

STYLE IS TOTALLY PERSONAL. In order to find what works best for you, it is necessary to pay attention to the details that create the style or look that you admire and add your own flair. Color, texture, and proportion are the three key elements of design that you should familiarize yourself with. I discuss these throughout the book but have provided additional details and some general guidelines below. After you have honed your eye to recognize and appreciate these elements, you'll receive an enormous amount of satisfaction and pride by putting them to use.

color

Color transforms our surroundings and alters our moods. Our reactions to color exceed those of many other stimulants. Color can reflect personality, and it certainly reflects tastes.

So many people seem intimidated—even afraid—to use and especially to mix color in their home or attire. Perhaps this is a result of living in too many white rooms or having too many color choices and becoming confused. Or perhaps it is the fact that color is so much a part of our everyday visual vocabulary that we take it for granted and do not notice it. Georgia O'Keeffe expressed the art of seeing when she said: "Nobody sees a flower, really, it is so small we haven't time, and to see takes time, like to have a friend takes time." I apply the same sentiment to the understanding of color. Consciously observing and assimilating color and color combinations requires time and discipline. While we absorb our surroundings subconsciously, this is not enough to refine and develop personal style.

By spending so many years as an art student and a clothing designer, I can honestly say I have worked and consciously created with color most of my life. In fashion one of my greatest delights was creating exciting and unusual color combinations. Therefore, I am astounded when I read some of the ridiculous dictates on color, concerning makeup, fashion, interior design, and even flower arranging. These rules are absurd and often change with the wind. However, there are some classic guidelines and basic information on color theory that can provide the necessary foundation on which to build.

Volumes have been written about the science and the use of color—but none of us has the time, or probably the interest, to plunge into pages of color theory. What then is the best way to learn about the effective use of color? By looking! The two best and, for that matter, easiest ways to explore color are to study great artists and to observe nature—the real expert.

While there are many great artists with a beautiful color sense, there are a handful that I frequently refer to as my personal color

elements of style

guides. Foremost is Matisse with his fresh, bold combinations of color. The colors he used and combined provide a wealth of information for flower arranging. Eighteenth-century painters, such as Boucher, Watteau, and Fragonard, are wonderful sources for the mid-range of soft pastels. One of my favorite painters, Zurbarán, is a great reference for rich jewel tones. Twentieth-century artists, such as Kandinsky—who also wrote about color—and David Hockney, are also tremendous sources of color inspiration.

Some of the most direct inspirations for color and flower arranging are the beautiful Dutch flower painters of the seventeenth century. Redouté, known for his beautiful renderings of roses and other flowers, also painted in the manner of the Dutch flower masters of the sixteenth and seventeenth centuries. Eighteenth-century France represented the

pinnacle of the decorative arts in Europe, during which color reached levels of refinement that have rarely been surpassed.

Whenever I visit a museum or an exhibition I buy postcards of the paintings and drawings that affect me. After years of doing this I have a collection of postcards that I periodically leaf through for inspiration. Sometimes before a large dinner or party I pull out my color flash cards to soak up and refresh my color sense.

We all gaze at beautiful nature scenes and try to memorize them, but it

is so difficult. Therefore, I have taken up photography with a vengeance. If this doesn't appeal to you, visiting gardens or looking at magazines like *National Geographic* are also wonderful ways to absorb the colors that thrive in nature.

Cutting out pictures from magazines and keeping a file of pleasing images, ideas, or color combinations are great ways to create your own reference collection. I have done this since I was a child (starting in 1963 with Christmas cookie recipes from *Family Circle*). Whenever I see an image that enchants me—be it a display of food, a garden, or a faraway place—I put it in my file. I leaf through this maybe once or twice a year and use what catches my eye or sparks my memory.

To fully appreciate and utilize color, it is necessary to be familiar with the rudiments of color theory. Without getting into the science of color, each primary color (red, blue,

and yellow) has a secondary color (green, orange, and purple) directly opposite them on the color wheel. Since the secondary color enhances the primary color, it is also known as a complement. Specifically, the complement of red is green, the complement of blue is orange, and the complement of yellow is purple. When primary and secondary colors are mixed, all of the resulting colors create a series of color schemes that are either monochromatic, analogous, tertiary, clash, complementary, or split complementary.

Complements enhance one another and create vibrant and exciting combinations. All the tints (the color plus white) and shades (the color plus black) of these colors are also complements—so pink, a tint of red, and a soft celadon, a tint of green, are complements of one another. Below are more examples of complementary color schemes.

Brilliant red dahlias are vibrant against the border of vivid green viburnum

Color allows us to create and to express

leaves on page 175.

Another red-and-green combination on page 243 demonstrates how a deeper red (the apples) and a deeper green (the pine) are a more subtle combination of these colors.

Electric blue delphinium and bright coral orange sweet peas work as complements as do the deeper tones in the pattern of the English vase on page 125.

Purple violets and pansies contrast with bright lemons for another complementary scheme on page 65.

A complementary color combination with more subtle colors is shown on page 57. The deep purple tulips and soft yellow freesia are a more sophisticated and unusual complement. Even the exotic ranunculus are purple and yellow.

Analogous colors create yet another category of color schemes. Analogous colors are any three touching, or contiguous, colors on the color wheel. Red, yellow, and orange are analogous; blue, purple, green, blue

violet, turquoise, and chartreuse are analogous; and pink, coral, and soft yellow are analogous. As with complementary color schemes, analogous color possibilities are limitless and lively.

Pictured on page 131 is a beautiful array of analogous colors in the burnt orange container and luscious garden roses. Soft oranges, corals, apricots, and yellows create a warm and beautiful bouquet.

Another group of analogous colors are pictured on pages 28–29. Blue and green hydrangeas, green viburnum, blue Muscari, and purple anemones and freesias are "cool" analogous colors. Throwing in the bright yellow roses highlights the purples in the bouquets.

Monochromatic color schemes are created with one color and its tints and shades, as illustrated by the bouquet of lilacs on pages 88–89. Light and dark shades of purple texture this

bouquet beautifully.

A color can evoke totally different moods and reactions depending on its setting or how it is combined. For example, chartreuse is certainly not a universally liked color, but I find it a perfect foil for practically every color. On pages 36–37, chartreuse viburnum with deep purple violets and clematis create a bold but cool image; adding the brilliant cerise ranunculus to the bouquet instantly makes it more vibrant. For an even livelier bouquet, I use brilliant magenta and chartreuse zinnias to create a gay and summery arrangement on pages 148–149. A soft tint of chartreuse accents peach ranunculus and roses on pages 20–21 in a softer and

more romantic arrangement.

Finally, a subtle but beautiful tactic is the employment of just one color. For example, instead of using only one red— use two, three, or more hues, tints, and shades of red. In the bouquet on pages 228–229, I've combined a true red, a blue-red, and an orange-red to create an effect of shadow, light, and texture. It looks "red" but because of the subtle difference in shades, the effect is less static and therefore more exciting. The same theory applies to the use of multiple whites in the bouquet on pages 246–247. These multiple shades and tints of white (bluish white, greenish white, and a warmer white tinged with yellow or rose) combine to make elegant yet interesting arrangements.

Color allows us to create and to express ourselves, our tastes, and our personal style. So pick your favorite colors and do not be afraid to experiment— the rewards will be great.

ourselves, our tastes, and our personal style.

Interesting texture can be created with a number of elements. Subtle combinations of flowers, leaves, and berries make interesting focal points as do flowers of the same species but of varying scales—a full-blown garden rose, a tighter mid-size rose, and a spray of miniature roses. Mixing various surfaces can

texture

also produce a richer look as the shiny ilex berries against the velvety petals of the roses and the deep rich petals and color of the amaryllis do on pages 226–227. Opaque and translucent petals work

beautifully together to add depth to an arrangement. Of course the designs of the flowers themselves, such as the carnation with its saw-tooth edge, also create texture as the petals of one flower nestle against

those of another.

Many types of foliage and berries add textural dimension. Foliage, such as eucalyptus with its silvery leaves and cascading berries, gives a sense of depth and movement. Developing your sense of texture will help you create more interesting bouquets.

In the old school of floral design one measured the distance between flowers and built pyramids and shapes to create "harmony" or "disharmony." The rule was that the bouquet should be one and a half times the size of the container. I have nothing against trends of "floral decoration" or these "principles of design," as they can often be useful. However, the best

proportion

results do not come from a list of archaic edicts but rather from choosing the most beautiful flowers, arresting colors, and interesting textures and arranging them in a suitable container and environment.

The two most important elements when working with

proportion are: the scale of the flowers in relationship to the container, and the arrangement's scale in relation to its purpose and placement within your home. Always keep surroundings—the height of the ceiling or the size of the table—in mind.

I feel that bouquets are

often too demure. Naturally, one does not want to obstruct eye-contact at the dinner table, but there are many ways to create a memorable bouquet. Try to avoid being safe all the time. Safe is a hairsbreadth away from boring and utterly forgettable. If in doubt, go a bit overboard. Better to make an impact with your flowers than to have them go unnoticed.

Look and study the work of those florists,

putting it all together

friends, or artists that you admire. Whenever you see a bouquet, a table setting, a painting—or anything for that matter—that you admire, think about why it pleases you. Is it the color or combinations of color? Is it

the size of the bouquet or how it looks in a certain container? Is it the composition of materials and colors such as the tablecloth or table accessories?

Every artist has studied and learned from the work

of other artists, whether in the fine or applied arts. Learn to consciously look, absorb, copy, and experiment. Eventually your own style will emerge through the beautiful bouquets that you conceive and create.

containers

Containers are critical to the overall look of a flower arrangement. My grandmother began teaching me about the important relationship a flower has with its container at an early age. She explained the significance of setting, occasion, lighting, and surrounding colors in determining the final look of the arrangement and the appropriate container. For example, a formal bouquet in a rustic basket looks funny—like pairing brown leather shoes with a black lace cocktail dress. Exciting juxtaposition of container

and flowers is interesting, but wrong, disparate elements are simply jarring.

Anything that holds water is a container. We all have varied tastes and budgets to work with, and these factors determine what types of things one collects. Your collection should represent your taste, be it modern, formal, rustic, traditional, minimal, or grand.

Your vases and flowers should reflect your life and style. I have been collecting containers for years and I have a tendency to horde—I

still have inexpensive vases (and I do mean inexpensive) from my first bachelorette apartment. Every year I get the urge to pare down and simplify my life, but the bric-a-brac conjures up memories and I end up inventing reasons to keep everything. My pack rat nature came in handy as I was writing this book though, and I was grateful for my stockpile of containers.

If you do not have Grandmother's antique silver vases or cannot afford Baccarat crystal vases, there are

still limitless possibilities. I mix my antiques with inexpensive but alluring containers. Nowadays there is a vast range of reasonably priced antique reproduction styles and great-looking modern shapes. As an example, throughout this book I have spoken of my love for blue-and-white porcelain and ceramics. I have a rather large collection that consists of eighteenth-century Dutch delft, English stoneware, and nineteenth-century Chinese porcelain that I mix with my thirty-dollar vases from Taiwan. It all works together and looks terrific.

1

2

5

Consider the style of the container. Is it formal, rustic, sophisticated, ornate, modern, naive, or basic?

How appropriate is the container to the setting in terms of style, size, and color?

How complementary is the container to the flowers in terms of style, size, and color?

Do the flowers work with the texture, design, or pattern of the container?

What type of mood do you wish to create?

The backbone of your container collection should include vases with a relatively wide—but not too wide—neck or opening (three to four inches). This size will accommodate a number of flowers but is not so large that they will end up swimming in the container.

A frog, block of oasis, or a ball of chicken wire at the bottom of large containers will help control big arrangements. A grid of florist's tape over the mouth of the vase will lend additional support to stems and branches.

Baskets, wooden containers, horn, terra-cotta, and other unglazed pottery require a liner. Metal

liners can be hard to find, so I use plastic dishes from the kitchen. Line baskets with moss and set the container down inside.

Wash your vases and containers between uses with water and bleach. This kills germs and bacteria that shorten the life span of flowers. Detergent and soap do not accomplish this.

Think of everything

as a possible container. You do not have to have a rare eighteenth-century piece of porcelain to have an exciting and beautiful arrangement.

Silver shortens the life span of flowers, but I can't resist using it. It is beautiful, elegant, and complements almost every flower.

1. From eighteenth-century Georgian silver to inexpensive plate, silver is magical with flowers. My most basic and most utilized containers are silver or silver plate in simple shapes.

2. I collect late-eighteenth-century and Regency period Irish and English cut glass. Their graceful forms range from simple to complicated geometric patterns. Flowers require more care when arranging them in these transparent containers, as the stems and the clarity of the water will be seen.

3. I always try to place flowers that are in a colored-glass container in front of a window or with the light behind them. The true beauty of the glass emerges when light passes though it.

4. So many countries have created fabulous blue-and-white porcelain, china, and pottery—China, Portugal, England, France, and Holland being the preeminent masters. I have yet to find a color that is not complemented by blue and white.

Pictured here are just a few types of blue-and-white ceramics: English mason's ironstone; English transfer ware; Portuguese pottery; nineteenth-century Chinese porcelain;

late-eighteenth-century Dutch delft, and modern inexpensive pieces made in China and Taiwan.

5. I occasionally use baskets for bouquets of flowers. Nothing captures autumn like big baskets filled with apples, pumpkins, and gourds.

6. Dozens of terra-cotta pots, wire baskets, old sap buckets, and French water cans fill my greenhouse. Terra-cotta is a beautiful background for all colors. Try to find old terra-cotta pots, as they have so much more allure than the characterless modern shapes of today. A favorite shape of mine is the English Long Tom flower pot. I have a couple of old wire baskets that I love to use. Luckily, the pretty filigreed Victorian ones are being reproduced today at very reasonable prices.

7. During my first summer in Weatherstone I started collecting English majolica. This type of gay-colored pottery looks wonderful with flowers. The colors are so bright and pretty and lend themselves to a country setting. While most of the majolica is from the late nineteenth century, one can now find new issues of some of the more classic patterns and styles, such as the Wedgwood Green Leaf pattern.

8. Painted English porcelain and pottery make colorful and interesting holders for flowers. Using them necessitates extra consideration in terms of

color and style when selecting your flowers, since these figurative containers have their own strong personalities.

9. All that glitters is not gold, but even the imitation stuff can really dress up a table. I love the luster and light that gold and silver reflect. Candlelight and metals are magical together. Vermeil, the gold of porcelain de Paris, bronze doré, and brass are the classic gold finishes. Of course, not everyone has access to bronze doré, but there are now many talented potters who are working with gold finishes that do not look cheap or gaudy. Museum shops are a good source for these decorative items.

10. An assortment of nineteenth-century English Parian ware and bisque pitchers make wonderful containers for country bouquets. Their color-and-white patterns provide great foundations for virtually any floral color combination.

11. In New York I have a small collection of Russian and Swedish Pophery. The clean lines and neutral colors are bold and elegant and enhance the flowers. In the same sophisticated style, Japanese bronzes complement any color or flower with their simple form and beautiful patina.

12. For the country I like these rustic oak-and-silver containers. The horn-and-silver beakers are charming vessels for fall and winter bouquets.

basics

The single most important thing that you can do for your flowers is to pick and condition them properly. They will repay you by looking better and lasting longer.

Be sure your vases are really clean by washing them out with a chlorine-based bleach and water after each usage. If the glass becomes cloudy then clean it with the bleach solution and a scrubbing brush or old toothbrush. Shake and rub some sand, fish gravel, or clay kitty litter onto the surface to remove any film.

Prolong the life of your flowers by changing the water and recutting the stems often. It also helps to add a floral preservative or sugar (1 teaspoon to 1 quart of water) and a drop or two of bleach to kill any bacteria.

If the arrangement allows, turn it every day so that a different side faces the sun, otherwise some flowers (such as tulips) will twist toward the sunlight. The flowers will last much longer in a cool room away from hot radiators or drafts.

picking

The best time to pick flowers is early in the morning or, failing that, in the cool of the evening. Plants picked in the heat of the day are always slightly stressed and wilted.

Use sharp clippers to cut woody material, and sharp scissors or a knife for the softer stems. The moment flowers are cut, place them in a bucket with a few inches of lukewarm water. Take them back to the house quickly for conditioning and do not try to collect too many at once.

If you prefer to pick into a basket, do not overfill it. Collect a few flowers at a time and make frequent trips back to the house with your harvest. Have suitable containers ready with about six inches of clear water in them.

Spring flowers, violets, bulbs, and ferns take their conditioning water tepid (below 100°F).

Most other flowers respond best to warm water, which is more easily absorbed and carried up the stem (between 100°F to 120°F).

Woody-stemmed plants and material from trees and shrubs need hot water (150°F is fine). These include roses, hydrangeas, lilacs, crab apples, mock-oranges, and flowering cherries.

1. Recut the stem of each flower at a 45-degree angle about two inches above your first cut. If you cut straight across, there is a danger that the stem may rest flat on the bottom of the vase and the water won't be able to enter. Be sure that your scissors or clippers are sharp. If they are not, they will bruise the cells and water won't be able to travel up the stem. I find it unnecessary to cut the stems under water but put them in water immediately after cutting.

2. Remove any thorns on the stem, so they won't catch on

conditioning

other plants and make it difficult to move the stems around in the vase. Cut off any leaves that will be below the water line. This will prevent bacteria from multiplying in the water and clogging flower stems.

3. Place the stems in the container of conditioning-temperature water and spray the flower heads with cool water. Once the container is full, carry it to a cool, shady

place and leave it for several hours or overnight for the flowers to drink and the stems to become turgid with water.

Hard, woody-stemmed plants such as flowering shrubs, tree cuttings, and some perennials like chrysanthemums need extra attention:

Slit the bottom of each stem two or three inches up the stem. Two cuts will help the plant take in water. Some arrangers hammer the stems

instead, but I feel that this damages the water-carrying cells and is probably counterproductive. Continue with step 2.

For hollow-stemmed plants such as daffodils, zinnias, dahlias, heliotrope, and poppies:

After recutting the stems at a 45-degree angle, wipe off the white sticky sap that oozes from the stem. Sear the bottom of the stem with a match or candle flame for thirty seconds. This stops the sap from clogging the water tubes, which causes them to die. Continue with step 2.

special care

AMARYLLIS

Turn the hollow stem upside down and fill with water fortified with a floral preservative and plug with cotton.

ASTILBE

Pick when fully open; split stem ends.

BABY'S BREATH

(Gypsophila) Cut both annual and perennial varieties when they first open. Condition in cold water overnight.

BLEEDING HEART

Cut when four or five florets show color; scrape the bottom inch or two of the stem.

CARNATION

Pick when half to fully open. Recut at a 45-degree angle between the nodes. After conditioning, place in cold water for an hour before arranging in warm water.

CENTAUREA

(bachelor's button) Pick when three-quarters to fully open. Scrape the stem ends, split, and condition in warm water.

CHRYSANTHEMUM

Cut when flowers are completely open. Recut and recondition every few days

in warm water.

CLEMATIS

Sear the stem ends with a flame, or place in a half inch of boiling water for thirty seconds.

COSMOS

Pick before you can see the pollen, or force the buds as they begin to swell. Split the stems.

DAFFODIL

Cut the stem and hold it over a candle or gas flame to sear the end and stop the flow of sap.

DAHLIA

Cut when fully open, sear, and condition overnight in warm water. Before placing in the conditioning water, prick a whole in the neck of the stem with a pin to prevent air lock.

DELPHINIUM

Cut when half of the flower spikes show color. Pinch off the top buds as they do not open once cut. Always place in water fortified with plant food.

FORGET-ME-NOT

Split stems and condition overnight in cold water.

HYACINTH

Cut off the white part of the stem, sear the bottom, and prick the neck of the stem. Do not spray with water; it will turn the flowers brown.

IRIS, GERMAN

Cut when the first bud is nearly open. Add plant food to vase.

LILAC

Cut when flowers are half to fully open. Scrape the stem two inches from the bottom, and make one or two long slits in it.

Condition in hot water at 120°F to 150°F.

LILY

Cut as the first bud opens, taking no more than one-third of the stem, or next year's bulb will not mature. Remove the stamens with scissors or the pollen will stain your skin and fabric.

LILY OF THE VALLEY

Cut when the top buds are still closed.

MARIGOLD

Cut when flowers are fully open. Scrape stems and condition overnight.

PEONY

Cut anytime from once the bud has colored to when it is fully open. Scrape and split the stem, and plunge it into deep hot water for four hours. Condition in cooler water.

PHLOX

Cut above the node when half of the flowers are open.

RANUNCULUS

Stand in warm water for several hours.

ROSE

Scented roses are reputed to have a shorter life in the vase. Pick when the first two petals begin to open and condition as a woody plant. Recut at a 45-degree angle and split the stem a couple of inches from the bottom. If their heads are drooping, wrap the entire bunch in wet newspaper and either float them in water or place them in a deep bucket of water up to their necks for several hours. Remove from the water and strip off all the leaves below the container water line. Take off the thorns and condition as normal. Mist the heads with cool water and move to a cool place.

TULIP

Cut off the white part of the stem at a 45-degree

angle. Wrap the bunch in stiff, nonabsorbent paper up to the necks and place in deep, tepid water for several hours. Remove the leaves and place the stems in six inches of room-temperature water. To resuscitate drooping heads, prick the stem just beneath the flower with a pin to fill any air locks. Place back in the room-temperature water. Mist with cool water.

VIOLET

Cut when flowers are half to fully open. Soak the

whole flower—including petals—in cool water for a half hour. Wrap in a damp towel and refrigerate (do not freeze) for two to three hours.

YARROW

Pick when half of the flowers are open. Remove all foliage—it almost always wilts.

ZINNIA

Cut when almost fully open. Take off nearly all the leaves. Sear the stems with a flame for thirty seconds.

index

CREATING THIS BOOK was a wonderful, exciting, and fun experience for me, but as with any large project one person cannot do all the work. I would like to give my thanks to those whose hard work and dependability made this book possible. Some of these people were directly involved with the process and others were confidence builders and great cheerleaders. I am indebted to all my friends, employees, and the staff at HarperCollins for giving me so much of their time and support.

To Placido, the hardest working "can do" person I know. To Mittie Ann who religiously counted every flower for each bouquet, kept records on everything, and was a constant bright and optimistic presence. To Margarida, always sweet and upbeat, who helped clean, prepare, and schlep the flowers. To Susan whose talent and ingenuity were indispensable. To Nancy whose great cooking kept us all going happily. To Terry, a great gardener and encyclopedic source of information. To Kathleen who had to decipher my chicken scrawl and helped organize all the photo shoots. To Eddie who transported flowers hither and anon.

To Toby who organized the first draft of the manuscript. To Carl, the friend who had to listen to my constant chatter about the book and always encouraged me. To Mom who has always been my "you can do it" cheerleader.

To Doug Turshen who, despite his busy schedule, believed in the book and created the most beautiful graphics for it, throwing all of his talent into this project without a moment's hesitation. To Beth Bortz, my editor, who had the formidable job of cleaning up and organizing my rambling sentences into coherence and who walked this book through the publishing process. To Joseph Montebello for his amazing support, his vision, and his making my first publishing experience fantastic. To Rose Carrano and Kate Stark for their efforts in bringing this book to the right places. To the sales staff at HarperCollins for their efforts.

To Al Lowman, my agent, who got me to "the right publisher" and believed in me and my book from day one.

To Anna Wintour, whose taste and advice I respect, for her encouragement and help. To Annette and Oscar de la Renta for lending me the beautiful vases and objects from their home. To Bill Blass who allowed me to raid his glorious pantry for vases and dishes. To Alberto Pinto who gave me access to his beautiful belongings in Paris. To Henri and Domenique Moulie who taught me so much in such a short time at their beautiful flower shop Moulie Savart in Paris. To Sandy Mendelson and her crew who got the news out. To Joy Henderiks who introduced me to Henri and Sylvie and helped me so much in Paris. To Sharon Hoge who helped introduce the book across the country.

To Joe Armstrong who introduced me to Susan Goldberger, photo editor at *Garden Design*, and got me started with photographers. To Sylvie Becquet who through her beautiful work and dedication created so much of the photography in this book and became a friend in the process. To Alexandre Wolkoff whose great style helped me get the summer dance together. To Alan Richardson, a photographer and design director rolled into one whose talent I so admire. To François Halard, the great French photographer who took beautiful Parisian photos. To Melanie Acevedo whose talented eye set the standard of photography for the book.

To the great people in the flower markets: the ladies and gentlemen of Rungis in Paris, Hilary and Joe from Fisher & Page, Richie from Associated Flowers, and Richie and Gary from Gary Page. To the ladies at the New York Public Library who helped with resources.

To all of you, a million thanks.
Fondly,
Carolyne